Creating a Beautiful

Wedding

Victoria

Creating a Beautiful
Wedding

Hearst Books
New York

Library of Congress Cataloging-in-Publication Data
Victoria, the wedding book / by the editors of Victoria magazine.
         p.cm.
ISBN 1-58816-049-1 (formerly 0-688-11661-2)
1. Weddings - United States - Planning.
I. Victoria magazine (New York, N.Y.) II. Title: Creating a beautiful wedding.
HQ745.V53 1993   93-7347
395'.22—dc20   CIP

Text by Arlene Hamilton Stewart and Tovah Martin
Interior design by Nina Ovryn
Cover design by Diane Wagner
Front cover photograph by Robert Gattullo
Back cover photograph by Toshi Otsuki

Produced by Smallwood & Stewart, New York City

First U.S. Edition
2 3 4 5 6 7 8 9 10
Printed in Singapore

www.victoriamag.com

NOTICE: Every effort has been made to locate the copyright owners of the material used in this book. Please let us know if an error has been made, and we will make any necessary changes in subsequent printings.

CONTENTS

$\mathcal{F}$OREWORD

eddings are as beautiful and as individual as brides themselves. Every woman knows in her heart exactly how she wants the day on which she marries to be. There are so many enchanting customs to choose from, so many different ways to plan an occasion that is yours and your loved one's alone.

For most of us, marrying is a time when we weave our own desires with the traditions of our families ~ a happy blend, and a moment when all brides have a common bond. Following time-honored customs gives us a wonderful sense of continuity and confidence; adding our very own touches promises a refreshing new beginning. In this book we have gathered thoughts for all kinds of weddings. Here you can select from many ideas those that will make your special dreams come true.

Whether you choose a chapel wedding in summer when a few field flowers tied with a ribbon is all the bouquet you desire, or a formal church wedding with organ music heralding a processional of bridesmaids, you will find in these pages inspiration to make your marriage day perfect.

Nancy Lindemeyer

FOUNDING EDITOR, Victoria MAGAZINE

Creating a Beautiful

Wedding

Married:

Wednesday, June 1st, 1892,

Hattie W. Wheeler and Mr. W.

Chamberlain, at Orange, Mass.

Chapter 1

ℛOMANTIC

BETROTHAL

AND YES I SAID

YES I WILL YES

James Joyce

ith a simple question and answer, your

world has changed. Your engagement is the beginning of the process

of uniting your two lives, of announcing to the world as well as to

yourself your intention to share the future together. Traditionally,

this is a period used to make wedding arrangements. You will be

deciding what sort of a wedding you want and how your days will be

spent in preparing for that occasion ~ shopping, fittings, parties,

invitations, planning and more planning. You may very well be won-

dering how you will ever find the time to do everything.

This is also a time that can and should be very special for you as a couple. Perhaps the best gift you can give one another is to take time out for just the two of you, to reflect on the true meaning of your decision and on the joys its promises. In the midst of all the busyness surrounding you, find quiet moments to step back and appreciate the unique nature of this period in your life; in years to come, as you look back, your memories will be stronger, your love even deeper.

Betrothal today is a pledge to marry made solely from the heart, an exchange of everlasting love. But it was not always so. In the Middle Ages, the betrothal was a serious arrangement between two families, not just the bride and groom. It was much more an affair of business than of the heart. If the couple fell in love as well, then they were truly blessed. At the time of the betrothal, promises similar to wedding vows were exchanged, and often a ring was placed on the right hand of the bride-to-be. A

kiss confirmed the arrangement until the actual marriage could take place, sometimes many years later.

Dowries, like chaperones and calling cards, today seem like quaint relics from the past. But they remained a popular part

Wedding traditions turned treasures: For many the heart of the betrothal is a ring. Opposite, a gold band set with seed pearls is displayed atop a brocade pillow trimmed with an unusual Victorian acorn fringe. Above left, a happy couple peers out from a wartime wedding photograph. Below left, a proper paper bride, serenaded by a chorus of musical cherubs, was created by a Victorian bride from her own wedding memorabilia.

ments become that elaborate rules of behavior sprang up to guide the courting couple. The Victorians, who were enamored of symbolism and ever love-conscious, encouraged the exchange of rings or other tokens of affection. A gentlemen might win increased favor by presenting his intended with an engraved locket, silver and ivory hair combs, or soft kid gloves. A love-smitten lady in turn would search for the perfect gift for her beloved, perhaps cuff links and shirt studs, a gold pocket watch, or a key ring and chain.

of the engagement process even until the beginning of this century. Usually money or property from the bride's family, a dowry served the purpose of helping to establish the young couple in the world. So complicated could premarital arrange-

This custom is as charming for today's couple as it was for yesterday's. Gift-giving can be an essential part of expressing love. Take the time during your engagement to exchange gifts, big or small, that say "I love you."

⌒HE GIFT OF SHARING

If you feel you're walking on air, perhaps even overwhelmed with the excitement and euphoria of being in love, you are hardly alone. Certainly Queen Victoria felt the same way, when she wrote in her journal in 1839, "Oh, to feel I was, and am, loved by such an Angel as Albert was too great delight to describe!" Throughout the ages great writers, poets, artists, and statesmen have put pen to paper to express their sentiments on the subject of love and marriage. Returning to those words, exploring those passions, can give eloquent voice to your own happiness and emotions. Books that inspire, confirm, expand your shared feelings are especially enjoyable now. How delightful to sit before a crackling fire and read aloud the stories and histories of great love matches, to follow famous lovers through their courtships. The complete diaries of Queen Victoria vividly portray the intense love and passion she shared with her adored Prince Albert; the story of F. Scott Fitzgerald and his wife, Zelda, reveals the profound commitment these two dazzling figures of the 1920s offered one another. And who could not be moved by the lifelong devotion of Winston Churchill for his beloved wife Clementine: "My greatest good fortune in a life of brilliant experience has been to find you and lead my life with you," he wrote to her after fifty years of marriage.

Anthologies of the great romantic poets ~ Robert and Elizabeth Barrett Browning, John Keats, Percy Bysshe Shelley, Christina Rossetti, Sara Teasdale, Lord Byron ~ are a wonderful place in which to lose yourself in reverie. Finding the poems that remind you the most of your love can be a pleasant respite from your busy schedule. And copied on a fine heavy stock in your best hand, they become intimate keepsakes.

If you are accustomed to keeping a journal, you probably have already written pages about your new experiences and feelings. If not, now is the ideal time to start a personal diary, recording precious details that might otherwise get lost in the flurry of hectic days. If you would like to encourage your fiancé to enjoy this enriching experience as well, consider presenting him with a gift of a handsome diary stamped in gold with his initials, along with an antique fountain pen.

Sharing your favorite works of art with each other during this precious time, before social obligations mount, can mean an afternoon spent in a museum or

The glow of lamplight illuminates a peaceful scene as the bride-to-be reflects on the voices of great writers and poets on two topics that hold a special interest for her love and marriage.

◆

gallery you both love, an evening at a concert, long strolls through gardens at twilight. Every expression of creativity becomes glorified as you look through the eyes of love, both in the present and in future reflections. The more you allow yourselves to express the spiritual side of love, the richer your wedding experience will become.

In the future, when you think of this time in your life, what will be the memory that comes most vividly to mind? Is it the moment your liking turned to love, the evening you decided to marry, the dinner where you told your parents you were engaged, your grandfather's poignant gift to you? Memories are difficult to hold on to, but with care and tending they can be beautifully preserved.

The first flowers he gave you ~ you

might press and arrange them in a collage of your initials intertwined. Do you still have the ticket stubs from the best movie you ever saw together, or the first Valentine he sent you? Store these precious keepsakes in a "treasure box," a beautiful fabric-covered hat box or wicker basket lined in lace to protect these most special memories. Consider including a poem you wrote, even if only a few lines, about how you felt when you realized you would marry this man. Perhaps you could frame a watercolor of the meadow where he made you a halo of wildflowers, or create a culinary journal of the special meals you shared, the dinners you made for one another. A desktop montage of all your favorite photographs will grace your home as it surrounds you with the tokens of love that have made up your romance.

The present becomes the future in precious mementos: pressed flowers from your first corsage; sketches of romantic rambles, delicate monograms combining your initials.

◆

Has yours been a romance played out to music? Do you remember the first song for which you shared a passion? How wonderful to create a library of the music that has brought you closer together ~ glorious symphonies, lilting folk tunes, jazz quartets. Gather up a special keepsake edition of the recordings to share again and again on special occasions throughout your lives together.

If the outdoors is part of your spiritual replenishment, find the time for a walk through the woods to pick up pinecones or gather wild thyme; wade in a brook, go ice-skating on your lunch hour. You should return home refreshed, and a potpourri made from those pinecones, or a sachet made with your harvest, will extend the pleasure and the memories.

23

A ROMANCE
OF LETTERS

*E*lizabeth Barrett and Robert Browning: Theirs is one of the most heroic love stories of all time, a passionate and profound love borne by two great poets for each other. She was thirty-eight, the more famous writer, her gallant spirit masking enormous unhappiness caused by years of illness that eluded diagnosis and treatment. He was thirty-two, struggling to make his way through the London literary scene. Filled with admiration for

Elizabeth's work, Robert begged until he was allowed a visit with her. They met and fell in love. The rest is history ~ and literature ~ for when two great poets fall in love we are all the beneficiaries. From Robert, Elizabeth received "the most exquisite letters possible." In return, Elizabeth penned the famed *Sonnets from the Portuguese,* giving the world a new measure by which to count the ways of love.

As the eldest daughter in a household that was extraordinarily repressed even by

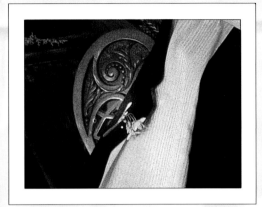

the standards of 1845, Elizabeth dwelt as a near-invalid in the sanctuary of her rooms in her father's home, until the day Robert Browning deposited his overcoat and hat in the hallway outside her door; the photographs above are re-creations of that first meeting. Their friendship grew at an astonishing pace, planting deep roots that nourished them the rest of their lives. Their secret courtship correspondence of over five hundred powerfully emotional letters not only sustained these two lovers, it has become one of literature's most exhilarating treasures.

Despite Elizabeth's certainty that her father would disown her, on October 11, 1846, she courageously eloped to Italy with Robert. Although they lived in exile, their marriage was deeply satisfying beyond their wildest wishes. It produced one son and some of their greatest works of art.

Mr. and Mrs. Samuel Flame

and

Mr. and Mrs. Howard Ehrlich

request the pleasure of your company

at the marriage of

Lana Susan Flame

and

Abraham Ehrlich

Saturday, the thirty-first of March

Nineteen hundred and ninety

eight thirty o'clock in the evening

The Equitable Tower

Seventh Avenue, fiftieth floor

Street, Galleria entrance

New York City

Black tie optional

Lisa B. Dubrow

and

David L. Charna

invite you to join them

at their wedding

Sunday, October 15, 1989

3:00 p.m.

Huppah will be raised at 3:30 p.m.

Scott Alan Gallery

27 Lafayette Street, second floor

New York, New York

cocktail celebration to follow

Glen

r. and Mr.
avour of a reply is requested by March 15th

ummer Night's Gathering

in us for a late garden supper

uddy and Pam Farnsworth

Satu uly twenty-first
at sunset

6 Circle Drive
Gler e, Long Island

))ITH PEN IN HAND

The happy task of attending to wedding correspondence starts with
choosing stationery and invitations. You
will be writing lots of notes, making lists,
organizing endlessly. To get in the mood,
find a spot just for special stationery, even if it is only a corner
of a bookshelf, and make it look
pretty and gay. Baskets or hat
boxes can hold note papers, invitations, replies, lists. A pretty
calendar marks the days. Antique
china cups filled with stamps look
charming. And a silver or hand-

*Filmy delicate
parchment, Italian
marbleized rag,
smooth and rough-
textured card stock,
these one-of-a-kind
papers heighten the
aura of any
wedding celebration.
Pressed with
flecks of roses, gold,
or ribbons, each
custom-made sheet
can be tinted to match
the bridal colors
and hand-lettered or
engraved.*

◆

carved letter opener becomes a permanent
keepsake of these peaceful moments. The
pleasure of writing is increased with a fine
fountain pen and quality inks.

A century ago, an engaged young lady
would retreat to her study or her desk,
take pen in hand, and start to work ~ she

would need wedding invitations, invitations to teas and at-homes, thank-you notes, calling cards. The etiquette-bound Victorians followed very prescribed social forms, so most brides of the period chose traditionally worded wedding announcements that were beautifully engraved in a classic type on a substantial white card stock, which the bride would then hand-address in her best script.

This kind of wedding invitation, with its classic appearance and formal wording, is still very much the choice of many of today's brides. Changes in family circumstances ~ invitations issued by both sets of parents, the bride and groom hosting the wedding themselves ~ can easily be accommodated by this graceful style.

If yours is a less traditional sensibility and you consider your stationery another part of your wedding ensemble, you may be drawn to colored paper stock and lettering styles that most reflect the mood you plan to create. Truly beautiful writing papers are available, handmade in textures smooth or rough, colors demure or bold, heavy in weight or light and translucent.

The phrasing of the invitation can also be a dignified and witty variation on the classical: elaborate or simple, poetic or traditional, serious or lighthearted, handlettered or printed. Perhaps you always loved the opulence of your grandmother's invitation and wish to capture the same spirit. Perhaps you want to include a few lines from a favorite sonnet or a sketch of a place you both love.

Often the size of your wedding influences the character of the invitation.

Special touches from the pen of the busy bride-to-be might include a hand-lettered scroll, like the one above, for her wedding guests to sign.

Engraved or printed invitations work best for large gatherings, while smaller weddings give couples more freedom to personalize the announcements. And any invitation penned in a calligraphic hand is supremely elegant. Calligraphy is especially handsome on a heavy paper, along with hand-lettered envelopes. A true romantic would then seal the envelope with a wax impression of the bride and groom's last initial. The consummate flourish would be to have invitations delivered by hand, each with its own fresh rose. The Victorians often embellished their

romantic correspondence with pressed flowers and leaves, paper-lace filigrees and hearts, satin and lace ribbons. For the unabashedly sentimental, these ideas can be adapted to wedding invitations as well. For dear friends who live very far away, a note announcing your marriage, perhaps accompanied by a smiling photograph of the two of you, would be a thoughtful way to show how much you care. Tucking a small message inside the invitation lets special guests know you hope they will celebrate with you.

In today's fast-paced world, handwritten notes are a most considerate expression of affection. Notes on beautiful paper asking your bridesmaids, flower girls, and maid of honor to be in your wedding party are gracious, as is a hand-written note to the person who will be performing the ceremony. But most of all, it is the thank-you note that will define you as a person of tender sensibility. Do not hesitate to go beyond letter-writing formulas and express yourself openly. That which is written from the heart is always appreciated, no time more so than now.

LINKING THE GENERATIONS

What is it about having a wedding of our own that makes us fascinated with all weddings? It is a phenomenon that most brides experience ~ bridal magazines catch our eye at the newsstand, the wedding announcement section in the newspaper is the first page we read. Not only do we delight in all kinds of information about the weddings of famous people, but the nuptials in our own family suddenly seem completely compelling to us.

One family's keepsakes include a handwritten marriage agreement in an old-fashioned script; a silver mirror in which a new bride might have fastened her hair with a jeweled comb before sitting for her wedding photograph; and a hand-painted register in which important dates were recorded and family history preserved.

Engagements are times of change and preparation for a new life. Visits with family can illuminate the path to this new life. The older generations have so much to offer ~ what could be more pleasant and rewarding than spending an afternoon together pouring over family albums and Bibles, old portraits

and memorabilia? It is especially enjoyable now to learn details about other family weddings: Were they grand affairs, or were they held at home? How were the brides dressed? What were the receptions like? What kinds of foods were served? Do the recipes still exist? Some careful family research may reveal a great deal about the loves, hopes, challenges, and accomplishments of your ancestors. This will enable you to see your place in the family more clearly, appreciating all that has come before you.

There was a time when your heart belonged only to Daddy. Here it is captured forever in a photo on your mother's dresser. Happy portraits old and new trace love through the generations. Heavy silver frames add a special luster.

Your trip back in time may spark off ideas for your own celebration. If the flower girl from your mother's wedding is a guest at yours, why not give her her own special bouquet and toast? How about including a very senior member of your family, or the groom's, as an attendant? Suffragette Lucy Stone was a bridesmaid at age eighty-two. Who was the best man at your father-in-law's wedding? Perhaps he would like to make a toast to the son and daughter-in-law of his dear friend. A family member's turn-of-the-century wedding certificate, elaborately engraved and beautifully scripted, could serve as a model for yours.

A Marriage
Of Two Families

More than a marriage of two people, a wedding brings together two families. A new group is created, unique in its character and complexity. To commemorate this extended family, what could be friendlier than a gathering at dinner? What could be more cordial than the sight of a dining table so beautifully set that it says "Welcome!" right down to the last glowing taper?

To many traditionalists, the etiquette of this first family dinner dictates that the groom's family make the overture about hosting the get-together. But because modern hospitality knows no such boundaries, it is perfectly fine for the invitation to be issued by either side. And while hosting a meal in a restaurant has its charms, there is nothing more gracious than opening one's home on such a special occasion.

Dinner is a delightful combination of favorite recipes from both families. The sharing of this meal is as nourishing as all its wonderful dishes. Across the generations and across the table, deep bonds are forged as these two families begin to become one.

A BRIGHT GOLD RING

With this ring . . . Surely these are words engraved on every bride's heart. The wedding ring is a powerful symbol, a constant reminder of a couple's love and commitment to each other ~ love with no beginning and no end, a little piece of eternity.

The tradition of the ring is as old as the rite of marriage itself. The earliest betrothal rings were made of bronze, ivory, or bone, and were given to the bride-to-be as an indication of the man's intent. This ring was worn on the third finger of the right hand, transferred over to the left during the actual marriage ceremony. (The practice of wearing a ring on the third finger of the left hand appears as early as ancient Greece, when it was thought that the nerve of that finger had a direct connection to the heart.) Later, in the Middle Ages and the Renaissance, rings were fashioned from iron as well as gold and silver, in plain and simple designs or glistening with diamonds and other precious stones. Double or triple interlocking bands, known as gimmel rings, were popular; one piece was given to the prospective bride and one to the groom, to be reunited at the time of the wedding ceremony. Since the seventeenth century, the thin gold band has reigned supreme. The romantic Victorians added their own poetic touch by engraving personal inscriptions, such as *Ever Thine*, inside the band. How lovely to replicate this tradition with your own initials or thoughts.

So inventive were Victorian jewelry makers that lucky brides had their choice of many romantic designs. The "hidden heart" ring, which could be separated to reveal a tiny heart within, was popular, as were other symbols of unity: hands and hearts clasped together, tied bows, and buckles. A gold coiled snake with jewels for the eyes became the most desirable wedding ring of all when Queen Victoria became a royal bride.

Wherever it is worn, whatever its style, price, or provenance, the wedding ring is the piece of jewelry every bride most treasures and loves.

A pair of graceful Victorian wedding bands exhibits fine workmanship that only improves with the passage of time. Gold and platinum have always been popular choices, from the simplest gold bands to these intricate designs. Their beauty makes it difficult for the bride-to-be to choose one favorite.

ᗞEAR FRIENDS

Amid the hustle and bustle of the wedding preparations, it is comforting to have friends to call on when things become overwhelming. It is easy to become preoccupied now; perhaps the best antidote is to take a moment to spend with good friends. Give yourself the gift of time; find little corners in your week for visits and chats on the telephone.

Thoughts of friendship will be very much on your mind as you assemble your bridal party. The role of maid or matron of honor is reserved for a loving ally who will share in preparation details and stand by you as you take your vows, acting as both witness and joyous celebrant. What comfort and pleasure to be surrounded by your dear friends at such an important time.

The face of friendship gazes out, always steady, always reassuring. Whether by your side or in your heart, friends help us understand the meaning of life's journey. Now, of all times, intimate conversations keep friends close to you. Letters to those far away help focus your thoughts as well as share them.

◆

ᘎHE BRIDE'S TEA PARTY

I f you were a bride in Victorian times, you would probably invite your friends to a tea party to ask them to be in your wedding. It would be a gay occasion, with homemade cakes, lacy tablecloths, your best silver. You would bake a sweet white layer cake, taking care to hide inside it charms symbolizing different faces of love: tiny silver rings, horseshoes, hearts, anchors, thimbles, crosses. And before your guests departed, you would give each a gift of appreciation.

Enchanting Victorian lace cases, sewn by the bride herself, or perhaps by a bride long ago, make charming keepsakes for the wedding party. Fashioned from lace handkerchiefs or pieces of antique lace, these lovely cases will cosset lingerie, stockings, even love letters.

◆

If the nostalgic side of you demands expression, you could re-create this charming fête as a way to thank your friends for their kindness. Every bit as lovely would be a lunch party at a museum, garden, or historic estate, where you could present your friends with fine handmade or personalized gifts.

SHOWER
OF FRIENDSHIP

he ring of fine china, peals of laughter, mountains of wrapping paper, blushes and sighs – if you are lucky enough to be the guest of honor at a bridal shower, you will be sharing in a wonderful feminine ritual. The shower is a gift-giving occasion that has, to a large degree, replaced the bridal hope chest and often the engagement party as well. But more than an opportunity to equip your pantry and linen closet, the shower is an important part of the wedding celebration repertoire. And when looked upon as a time when women, married and otherwise, usually get around to sharing their innermost thoughts about men and marriage, it can be positively educational!

Surrounded by the most loving and supportive of friends, this is your chance to bask in the glow of an informal spot-

light, to sit back and let those closest to you delight in doing things for you. In sixteenth- and seventeenth-century Holland, when a young girl with no dowry wished to marry, practical Dutchwomen would gather forces and create a "shower" of household gifts for her that would serve as that dowry. Since that time the ritual of the bridal shower has endured ~ as a way for women to look after one another, to ensure that the new bride will have everything she needs to start her new life, to seize the opportunity to pass along valuable advice from generation to generation. And while the shower is basically a lighthearted celebration, and today is sometimes even a coed affair, it remains a rite of passage that brings the bride closer to the women in her life and makes the approaching wedding day even more of a reality.

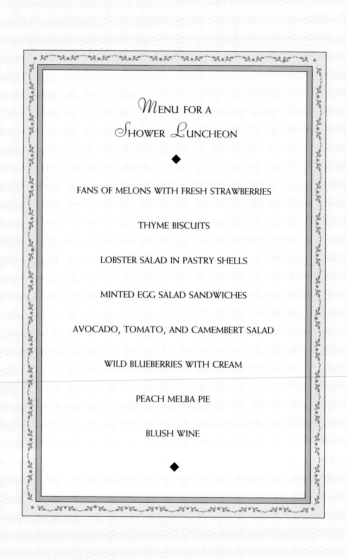

$\mathcal{M}$ENU FOR A
$\mathcal{S}$HOWER $\mathcal{L}$UNCHEON

◆

FANS OF MELONS WITH FRESH STRAWBERRIES

THYME BISCUITS

LOBSTER SALAD IN PASTRY SHELLS

MINTED EGG SALAD SANDWICHES

AVOCADO, TOMATO, AND CAMEMBERT SALAD

WILD BLUEBERRIES WITH CREAM

PEACH MELBA PIE

BLUSH WINE

◆

$\mathcal{I}$N GRATITUDE

During this romantic time, when good friends become dearest friends, when families draw even closer, there is still another occasion to celebrate. It is the rehearsal dinner, a time of high spirits, giddy anticipation, and perhaps a twinge of stage fright. Whether you are having a church ceremony that requires a somber rehearsal, or plan to say only a few well-chosen words before hosting a bridal breakfast at home, the evening before your wedding gives you a wonderful excuse to bring those closest to you together for an informal party. For such a festive occasion, nothing could be better than a menu that allows everyone to relax with party fare that is fun and easy to prepare ~ a hearty fish stew such as a cioppino, perhaps, served with lots of crispy herb

$\mathcal{A}$ peek through the curtains reveals a glowing dining room just moments before a rehearsal dinner. One can almost hear the sounds of laughter as the bridal party arrives from the rehearsal, ready to unwind before the big day. This is the perfect setting to salute friends and family with toasts by candlelight.

bread and salad. What a treat to top it off with a spectacular dessert ~ could there be anything more sumptuous than English trifle mounded high with layers of whipped cream, crunchy macaroons, sweet berries, and crème Anglaise?

Presenting gifts to your bridal party at the rehearsal dinner is a time-honored tradition. Whether your gifts are bear hugs or declarations of love, handmade presents or simply beautifully written letters, they let others know how much their love and support have meant to you. For the rest of their lives, your friends will look at the gold locket you

The art of gift-giving at its peak: opposite, a magnificent silver flacon, its heart shape a perfect declaration of love, and, above, an unusual jeweled cameo.

◆

had engraved with their initials, or page through the photo album you started for them, and think of you. It is especially nice to find something to add to a personal collection ~ a piece of American art pottery, a handmade twig basket, a delicate Staffordshire teapot.

This is also a time for your voice of thanksgiving to find expression. Gifts that say "I appreciate all you did for me" will always be cherished. A corsage of velvet violets is a pretty way to thank your aunt for the family pearls she is lending you for the wedding. For your cousin traveling hundreds of miles to celebrate with you, a small travel bag filled with hand-milled soaps and other miniature toiletries is a thoughtful gesture. What could please your wonderful dressmaker more than a lavishly illustrated book on the history of wedding dresses? The few lines you write to your mother and father tonight will speak volumes forever about your gratitude and love.

If you have already given your bridal attendants gifts at a private tea, remember them this night with a tiny box of the best chocolate truffles or the sweetest tussy-mussy of dried flowers, as everlasting as your regard. An object of beauty in itself, your wedding invitation, framed in gleaming heavy silver or ornately carved wood, makes a thoughtful gift for your parents and the groom's.

And then there is always that special friend, or perhaps your sister, the one you first confided your feelings to, the same person who told you that your husband-to-be was the right man for you to marry. What a happy debt that is to repay! You give her a scrapbook marking all the wonderful moments in your friendship, from Girl Scout badges you earned together to mementos from the trip abroad you shared.

A groom's tribute to his friends might include a fine antique. Vintage timepieces, right, and an etched wine decanter, above, are lasting ways to express friendship.

◆

Your fiancé has considered gifts for his friends as well ~ tickets to the Super Bowl, Babe Ruth's autograph, a first edition of *The Sun Also Rises*. When he turned to you for inspiration, you suggested something classic such as a crystal decanter, antique timepiece, or leather desk set. You love the painted silk ties he has chosen for his ushers, and everyone is moved by the poignancy of a long-forgotten childhood photograph of these old friends together, now framed in handsome ebony.

This evening you are very much aware that you both have been experiencing great happiness, and for that you could not be more grateful. Whatever ways you find to express that sentiment, whether with affectionate gifts, gracious hospitality, sincere notes, or eloquent nostalgic letters to friends, your thankfulness may encompass a wider orbit now as you move into a larger family and community life.

Chapter 2

B RIDAL
ATTIRE

A WOMAN

CAN NEVER BE TOO

FINE WHILE

SHE IS ALL IN WHITE.

Jane Austen

ust as every love affair has its own story, so does every wedding ensemble. It may be one of family love and honor as the bride walks proudly beneath her great-grandmother's veil. It may speak eloquently of a reverence for simplicity as vows are taken in a handmade organdy blouse worn over a long straight skirt. Or it could be a story that reaches back into history as the bride recaptures the joy of a nineteenth-century belle whirling into her new life in yards of rich satin. Piece by piece every bride puts together her ensemble until a beautiful whole emerges ~ family heirlooms more precious with each use, fine fabrics old and new, flowers of heartbreaking beauty. Veils, jewelry, gloves, shoes, lingerie, handbags ~ every detail is charged with meaning.

Long white dress, gossamer-like veil, delicate kid slippers, plump bouquet of roses: This is the classic bridal outfit. And while it may seem as though it has been popular forever, today's bride does not have to look too far back in history to discover its origins ~ the delightful, love-at-first-sight marriage of young Queen Victoria and her Prince Albert in 1840. Truly one of the world's great love matches, their wedding was as joyful as the feelings they shared for one another. By appearing in a stunning, extraordinarily feminine all-white ensemble, the

young queen broke with the tradition of royal brides who until that time wore robes of stately white and silver. The glory of her rich satin gown, her floor-length veil of the finest English Honiton lace, and her bouquet of orange blossoms, myrtle, and snowdrops all spoke of a highly romantic sensibility that characterized an era and began a custom that brides still follow to this day.

But the Victorian-inspired ideal is by no means your only option. Many beau-

Opposite, a bride could not be more glorious than in this splendid high-necked Victorian blouse with its inset of hand-wrought lace. Above left, the artistry of Victorian jewelry enhances any ensemble: drop earrings, delicate necklaces, gold lockets, filigree brooches. Below left, a pair of rare antique hand-embroidered slippers adds a footnote of elegance to the most romantic of gowns.

◆

tional formal satin gowns dusted with seed pearls in classic white. You can choose from a wider spectrum than ever before ~ glorious shades of ivory, ecru, mother-of-pearl, the most fragile pinks, yellows as fresh as butter or pale as the first glow of day, washes of blue and lavender ~ or perhaps even bright red. Added to all this are the flowers, from great elegant sprays of calla lilies to merry little nosegays, from baskets of wildflowers to creamy roses covering the family Bible.

Whether it is your first journey down the aisle or a return to married love; whether you choose an original designer creation, a treasure from your grandmother's attic, or a fabulous flea market find, you will surely find the ensemble that is exactly right for you.

tiful choices exist for you: crisp two-piece suits of linen, dreamy long-sleeved lace blouses with velvet skirts, pinafores of polished cotton, museum-quality heirloom dresses, beaded chemises that recall the 1920s, tradi-

SOMETHING BORROWED

For the bride who longs to be married in an authentic period wedding gown, a remarkable gift lies tucked away in the village of Amherst, New York. It is the Amherst Museum Heritage Wedding Gown Collection, the largest collection of antique wedding gowns in America. Each of the one hundred and fifty dresses from the past century and a half is magnificently preserved, and under the auspices of a unique loan program, a selection has been made available for a bride to borrow for her own wedding. In addition, a dress can be custom-fit if at all possible. To look like a vision from Victorian days, she can select from a dizzying array of sumptuous styles heavily frosted with laces, ribbons, trims, and bows. The handmade beauty of decades past is represented by rare two-piece ensembles that embody the Edwardian-era Gibson Girl look, delicate cotton batistes from the turn of the century, and sophisticated beaded chemises of the 1920s.

*V*INTAGE INSPIRATION

The enormous appeal of vintage wedding gowns is almost irresistible. Echoes of past eras and past lives, these fragile treasures are reminders of the enduring value and beauty of fine workmanship with their laces, embroidered flowers, fancy trims, and monograms.

Most hand-sewn clothing was tailored with large seam allowances, and in the hands of a skilled seamstress a vintage dress can look custom-made. Another idea is to combine vintage clothing with something new, such as a long flowing riding skirt with a new pair of high-button shoes, or a paisley shawl instead of a veil.

Preserving antique clothing requires care and loving attention. If you are calm and collected enough after the reception, check carefully for spots or stains, or assign this important task to one of your bridesmaids. Your grandmother might have removed a stain from her gown with a mixture of lemon juice and salt. Though gentle dabbing with a very mild liquid soap and water mixture may remove unfortunate marks, an item so precious as your bridal gown should be entrusted to an expert in the care of fine fabrics.

Upon returning from your wedding trip, line a large wardrobe box with leaves and leaves of fine tissue paper, preferably acid-free. Place your dress in the box and roll tissue pillows into the sleeves, then gently hold them on top. Fold the skirt under, then wrap loosely in unbleached, prewashed cotton or muslin. Store it in a dark, dry place away from extremes of temperature.

This beautifully preserved drop-waisted gown, opposite, is rich in vintage detailing. Above, a high-necked gown and matching veil of sheer net falling from a floral crown evoke 1920s elegance.

◆

THE LOVELIEST DRESS

While we acknowledge Queen Victoria for inspiring a century of allegiance to the all-white wedding ensemble, brides-to-be need feel no such restriction when selecting their wedding attire. This clothing completely transcends fashion rules and dictates; the only requirement is that it makes the bride look radiant.

A thousand years of history provides all the inspiration necessary. Elizabethan brides swore fidelity in brocades and velvets adorned with furs and jewels. This elegant, close-to-the-body style with its dropped waist and long narrow skirt still looks stunning today,

Above, a linen suit falls gracefully from pleats into scalloped borders of eyelet lace. Opposite is a whisper of a silk chemise by Norma Kamali, exquisitely detailed with intricate beadwork.

◆

completes the period feel. Two hundred years later, the Empire style of the eighteenth-century ushered in high waists and bonnets accented by precious handmade lace on jabots and fichus. This refined, modest fashion suggests drawing-room teas and embroidery by the fire. Jane Austen's Mr. Bennett would surely have approved of this look for his daughters.

But it was during the Victorian and the Edwardian eras when the wedding gown was elevated to the fairy-tale vision with which we are familiar. Exuberant skirts grew wider and wider to accommodate waterfalls of delicate hoopskirts and crinoline petticoats. Sleeves puffed out extravagantly. For evening, necklines plunged and bustles flounced through dreamy waltzes. Hair went up and drop earrings

especially for a winter wedding. In the summer, this look translates easily into dresses of filmy gauze and tapestry trim. Long, flowing hair entwined with buttercups

stretched into long dangling styles. High white evening gloves and square-toe satin slippers looked dazzling. Could anything be more romantic than off-the-shoulder insouciance for a bride who planned to dance the night away?

What may seem to be sumptuous excess was, to the bride of the late nineteenth century and early twentieth century, merely the fashion of the day. Rich detailing ~ braiding, pleats, ruching, flounces, and piping ~ covered every surface and every seam. Tiny waists, countless buttons and bows, bustles, and leg-o-mutton sleeves created the most feminine of looks.

$\mathcal{H}$ere is a bride who knew she wanted a highly romantic look and assembled it all perfectly. Her satin skirt, etched with embroidery, brushes the floor, falling into a magnificent train. Beneath a mass of upswept ringlets, her tiny drop earrings are perfect exclamation points.

◆

Perhaps yours is a sensibility that is fascinated by the more elegant and understated dresses that were introduced after the First World War. Chemises made their appearance, with shorter

sleeves or no sleeves at all, and a lower waistline. This is a charming silhouette with wide appeal. It seems to suggest a more worldly attitude, making it perfect for a more mature bride or a fashion sophisticate. And while this style looks good any time of the day, its great refinement makes it a perfect choice for late afternoon.

ℰlegance at its simplest, purest, most extravagant: This Christian Dior gown, swathed in yards of cotton tulle, is equally breathtaking from the front or back.

◆

The late 1950s saw the return of Cinderella in a magnificent fairy-tale wedding gown. Full-skirted, tight-waisted, jeweled and beaded, crowned with a tiara or elaborate headdress and veil, this is the gown that still grips our imagination. Ultrafeminine and timeless, it is always beautiful, afternoon or evening, in city or country.

There is so much to choose from that sometimes the possibilities seem staggering, especially if you are trying to assemble all the important elements into a whole: design, color, fabric, type of wedding, season, time of day. As you search for your own style ~ romantic, refined, glamorous, youthful or mature ~ you will have a wonderful guide: the knowledge that no choice you make from the heart could ever be wrong.

CROWNING GLORIES

It may float to the hem, spill out majestically into a train, reach the fingertips, or peek out from under a riding hat. It may be a square of priceless handmade Valenciennes lace or yards and yards of the simplest netting. It may cover the face, the shoulders, or just the corner of a twinkling eye. It can be either sheer or opaque ~ and it does not even have to be white.

The wedding veil is one of the most glamorous elements of the bridal wardrobe, but its origins are as enshrouded in mystery as the aura it creates. Many believe the earliest veils were cloth canopies under which a couple married. Later this practice may have evolved into a veil worn by the bride to protect her from unfriendly and envious stares. Centuries later, the veil

The unrivaled romance of a veil can transform even the most modest of wedding styles into a splendid statement. Here, a unusual tiara of silvered leaves entwined with pearls that gleam like moonlight will secure a length of fine vintage lace. The result will be romantic enchantment at its most powerful.

◆

reached its place of preeminence in the Victorian-inspired wedding. So taken was society with the great romance of the floor-length lace veil worn by Queen Victoria at her wedding that the veil was instantly adopted as the fashion of the day.

For over a century and a half, veils have been a permanent part of the traditional wedding ensemble, enchanting generation after generation of brides. In fact, they are so important to the bride that they are also thought to bring their own measure of good fortune. Wedding lore has it that because of the prohibitive cost of hand-made finery up until the mid-nineteenth century, borrowing a veil brought a bride special good luck, thus creating the ideal of "something borrowed" in the old wedding refrain of "something old, something new, something borrowed, something blue." Veils perform fashion magic as almost no other part of the ensemble, turning a merely wonderful bridal outfit into one of unforgettable splendor.

Brides who choose to marry in the morning or in the early afternoon enjoy great latitude in their choices. Veils can be tucked and gathered, held in place with antique hairpins or bursting radiantly from a crown. For ceremonies that take place late in the day or in the evening, long, long veils look especially dramatic.

More than just romantic fashion element, though, veils for some brides perform a protective function. Swathed under cascades of netting or lace, the

Above, a dreamy bride is tucked under a veil of tulle, bows, and pearls.
Right, a gossamer tulle veil flows from an antique gold chaplet.
Tendrils of stephanotis cling to its base.

◆

highly sensitive bride may allow all her feelings to wash over her, knowing that under her veil she has found a refuge.

No matter what time of day, season of the year, or degree of formality, every bride can indulge her most romantic side and envelop herself in the gossamer splendor of a veil. Worn decorously over the face as the Victorians would do, or thrown back to frame her face, the veil is a powerful symbol of bridal loveliness.

If you prefer not to include a veil in your wedding ensemble, a glorious headdress ~ from a simple wreath of daisies to a regal crown of jewels ~ may be the perfect choice. Headdresses have long been a favorite of European royalty; indeed, Anne of Cleaves married King Henry VIII in 1540 wearing a magnificent coronet of gold and precious gemstones tucked with sprigs of rosemary. Princess Alexandra of Denmark married Queen Victoria's son, Prince Edward (later King Edward VII), in 1863 with garlands of orange blossoms and diamonds in her hair.

There are many beautiful ways to recreate such royal radiance: an heirloom silver comb, a crown of dark red roses, a bouquet of beguiling pansies securing

Looking like the boldest, most confident heroine, a young bride rides right out of the pages of a Gothic novel and into our hearts. Who wouldn't fall in love with such a look? With the style and dash of a nineteenth-century equestrienne, this masterpiece is composed of the gentlest top hat abloom with pearls, roses, and soft satin bows, all wrapped in heavenly tulle. A sophisticated wing-collared linen blouse buttoned with pearls is the perfect foil for this high-spirited variation on a veil.

upswept hair. Experiment with a wreath of flowers mixed with herbs "for remembrance;" in winter, weave vines of ivy and myrtle through your hair, or sprigs of aromatic evergreens as lasting as your love. In spring, a straw bonnet looks delightfully unaffected trimmed with seasonal blossoms of hyacinths, freesias, tulips, snowdrops, or lilies of the valley. The glory of high summer brings with it a wealth of garden flowers to fashion into wreaths or wear in small braids: foxglove, Queen Anne's lace, old-fashioned roses, daisies, and Johnny-jump-ups.

For the unabashed romantic only: a procession of gardenias, opposite, intoxicates with their scent and beauty. Above, total immersion in orchids creates a look even a Greek goddess might have wanted for her wedding.

On the day of the wedding, your hairstyle is perhaps just as important as the clothing you have chosen. The right one enhances the mood of any wedding outfit as it heightens the drama and importance of the moment. It can elevate a subdued ensemble into one of glorious restraint or push an already romantic look into the stratosphere. Soft and satiny and romantic, bridal hairstyles must also be artful enough to maintain their composure through hours of celebration and posing for photographs.

The Victorians offered the bride a whole world of ornamentation and embellishment for the hair: piping, fringes, tassles, braids, as well as wreaths of their beloved orange blossoms. To create your own Victorian look, fasten upswept or backswept waves and curls with an antique or faux ivory comb. French braids, buns, and twists look elegant with more tailored lines, just as shining straight tresses look heartbreaking with the jeunesse of a sheer gossamer dress. Sometimes the simplest velvet headband is all that is needed

A duet of bridal looks to turn heads: Left, long shiny
tresses are brushed back and draped in a soft bow. Right, for the young
bridesmaid, a fairy-tale halo of peachy roses and white pear
blossoms shows off the beauty of her simple pulled-back hairstyle.

for a lovely daytime look; to transform it into an evening style, adorn it with diminutive flowers such as rosebuds or freesia attached with narrow picot-edged satin ribbon. Or take advantage of the power of opposites: A cascade of spirited corkscrew curls will stand in bold dramatic relief against the simplicity of a crisp linen suit; roses fashioned on a plain bar-

rette may be the understated sophistication you are looking for to pair with a French braid; an innocent organdy bow complements a sleek chignon.

For inspiration, consider turning to the charm of the hairstyles of an earlier era. How elegant it would be to wear your hair in a velvet turban, just as a bride in 1940 might have done. A snood fashioned

For the mother of the bride, left, elegant upswept hair
works wonderfully with her stunning vintage blouse. Right, a latticework
of hair woven with pearls is a beautiful sight on this bride,
whose curls dance about her face and fall gracefully down her back.

of lace with a corsage of camellias at the nape of the neck would be stunning with a full-skirted taffeta ball gown reminiscent of Scarlett O'Hara. A variation on an elaborate Victorian coiffure calls for hair piled high, fastened with hairpins, gentle tendrils escaping as if by chance.

Proportion and balance are other elements to be considered. A long, formal gown usually needs a more emphatic hairstyle than a shorter dress or suit. Dresses with high necks look wonderful with shorter upswept styles. Gowns with low or plunging necklines are beautifully balanced by longer, free-flowing locks. The natural beauty and drama of a bare back will be heightened by a hairstyle lifted high off the neck.

$\mathcal{G}$ENERATIONS OF JEWELS

$\mathcal{A}$cross the family and across the generations, jewelry boxes and chests are thrown open to prepare for a wedding day. Bracelets, necklaces, brooches, earrings, jeweled combs, and pins all come spilling forth to add their brilliant voices to the bride's ensemble. They might be family heirlooms, such as the pearls her great-aunt wore, or her mother's locket, or a cameo on loan from the groom's family. They could be newly found treasures that will always remain precious to her.

$\mathcal{A}$ potpourri of antique jewelry adds elegance to any wedding outfit. Here, a classic cameo, a diamond-studded brooch, and delicate drop earrings reflect the beauty of an earlier era with their high degree of detail and craftsmanship. Other choices include gemstones and pearls framed with lacy gold and silver filigrees.

◆

The intensified drama and emotions of a wedding call for explicit expressions of love, and today's bride is encouraged to show that affection in as many ways as she wishes. If she decides to wear her childhood silver charm

bracelet, we will admire her sentiment. If she drapes her grandfather's watch fob across her chest, we applaud her ingenuity. If she carries her grandmother's jet rosary, we know her soul is true and steady. Bridal jewelry is intensely personal, more like a prayer than a shout.

Because jewelry makers in the nineteenth-century were so creative and prolific, there are many beautiful pieces in existence. Cameos were a particular favorite of the Victorians. Today, they look especially graceful worn by brides as well as other members of the bridal party.

Even before the age of Victoria, it was customary for the groom to present his fiancée with a piece of engagement jewelry ~ a beautiful gold locket inscribed with both their initials, a fine seed-pearl necklace, a cameo, or crystals. Lavish or modest, this gift was cherished by the bride, who viewed it as a token of the very highest love and esteem. Often the bride would include this jewelry in her bridal ensemble. At her wedding, Queen Victoria wore a magnificent brooch, a large sapphire surrounded by diamonds, given to her as a wedding present from her beloved Albert. He in turn wore his gift from her, a diamond Star and Badge of the Most Noble Order of the Garter.

Precious stones set in a gold band became popular as a betrothal ring in the eighteenth century. Then, as now, these rings could be anything from simple settings with one or two pearls to elaborate creations encrusted with jewels. While the diamond ring reigns supreme, Victorian ladies considered engagement rings set with their birthstones to be the luckiest rings of all. What bride would dream of not wearing this precious token of love on her wedding day?

The opalescent beauty of pearls is as timeless as the tradition of wearing them on the wedding day. Opposite, nestled among swirls of French ribbon, is a simple strand of cultured pearls. Above, a magnificent antique cameo finds a perfect home on a pearl choker.

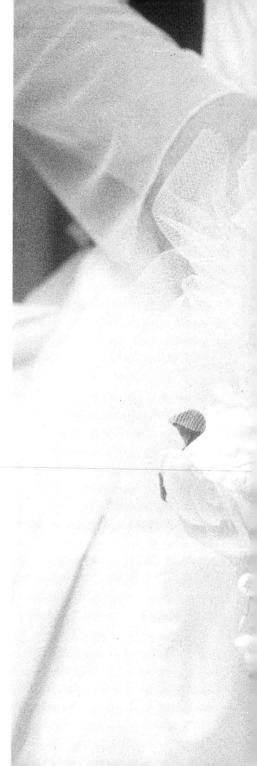

ℋEAVENLY BOUQUETS

Only blossoms can compare with the bride's own luminance. Petals echo the softness of a bride's cheek, freshly opened buds reflect her blush. Delicate floral scents are reminiscent of summer days of courtship, and floral perfumes preserve nuptial memories long after other recollections have faded. Even a modest bunch of daisies ~ long considered the flowers of innocence ~ gathered loosely in a piece of satin ribbon will add beauty to the moment. Just as every bride radiates her own special glow, every blossom has its own inner loveliness.

The bridal bouquet becomes a work of art in this classic tussy-mussy with a glamorous twist: Gilded vines of ivy provide a radiant counterpoint to a beautifully scaled arrangement. Full-blown roses, wide-open mums, pure white lilies of the valley, and chirpy ranunculuses make their own special contribution.

◆

Today, as the bride-to-be ponders her own bouquet, what glorious opportunities await her. She may anticipate the emotion of the day and play to it: sophisticated calla lilies for drama; a

simple nosegay of pansies for innocence;
a mix of phlox, ferns, and roses for a
country feeling. She may strike a dramatic chord with a single noble stem or an
armful of Queen Anne's lace fresh from
the meadow behind her house.

Certain flowers have traditionally
accompanied the bride on her journey
down the aisle. Brides of old carried
wheat sheaves and were crowned with
orange blossoms to symbolize the matri-
monial harvest. Rue, lavender, and rosemary snippets were strewn at the newlyweds' feet to ward off evil spirits, while
jasmine festooned the reception halls,
inviting angels to bless the union.
Perhaps because of their bell-shaped
throats or pure white petals, stephanotis,
calla lily, lily of the valley, sweet pea,
peony, orchid, and a host of other blossoms have joined the solemn ceremony.
Fragrance, of course, has always been the
most evocative of all considerations.

Floral traditions float poignantly
through families and cultures. In Europe,
the mother of the bride tucks sprigs of
biblical myrtle into the wedding bouquet.
The bride later removes the cuttings and
meticulously tends them until the day
when her daughter will walk down the
aisle. In the Middle East, artemisia, the

*Chrysanthemums are at the
heart of a classic white nosegay, top.
Above, pungent rosemary, thyme,
and sage are woven with deep red roses
and vivid lilacs.*

Top, frilly lace frames the most delicate lilies of the valley, roses, and stephanotis. Above, a formal mix of lilac, freesia, and foxglove is radiant atop a bed of ivy sprigs.

most acrid of herbs, is added to the nuptial nosegay, ensuring that love will endure bitterness as well as sweetness.

The Elizabethans put more emphasis on personal adornment than on decor and draped themselves royally in flowers. For the Victorians, the greatest floral creation of all was the nosegay, or the tussy-mussy, a small, sweet, plump bouquet. Brides poured all their love into this most intimate creation ~ a cushion of pansies, a round dumpling of hyacinths and roses, a tiny pyramid of the ever-present orange blossom. These nosegays were thought to be the ideal accompaniment to the intricacy of lacy nineteenth-century wedding gowns. They were hung with satin ribbon streamers knotted every few inches with flower buds to represent the steadfastness of love. Two knots symbolized the bride and groom; three represented their future child as well. A very sentimental bride would carry a small posy in one hand and a lacy handkerchief with the groom's initials in the other.

A larger bouquet, known as a chatelaine, also became popular in Victorian times. Traditionally made with a cluster of white roses ringed with maidenhair ferns, the chatelaine was also hung with satin streamers tied in knots. This roman-

tic style, still popular today, evolved into the long cascade. Dramatic sprays of flowers, usually all white ~ orchids, delphiniums, carnations, roses, lilies, dozens and dozens of each ~ spring forth in an elaborately constructed display that is rarely less than two feet in length.

Left, the supremely elegant shape of calla lilies plays off marble-smooth tulips in this bridal masterpiece. Above, a clutch of huge creamy tulips is the bridesmaid's version of the same bouquet.

For many brides, the all-white bouquet will always be a passionate favorite. Within this singular color choice lies a whole spectrum of subtle tones and shadings from which to choose: roses of ivory, ecru, antique damask, mother-of-pearl; orchids of crystalline white; pure-throated lilies of the valley; even blossoms with the most delicate lavender hue, from white hyacinths and delphiniums to one of the most beautiful bouquets of all ~ fragrant white lilacs tied with picot-edged satin ribbons.

Gala and gay or muted and sedate, flowers set an evocative bridal stage and keep the moment forever kindled in our memories. Garlands stretching into oblivion, petals strewn carelessly about, perfect blossoms presented to beloved family and friends ~ they all portray the many moods of a marriage.

THE LANGUAGE
OF FLOWERS

lowers have always mingled with romance. Since the beginning of time, tongue-tied suitors have offered clumsy posies as messengers of affection. A single blossom tossed in the path of a hopeful admirer is a universal sign of acceptance; a bouton-niere carelessly cast aside means refusal. For centuries, petals have been plucked to predict whether or not love is requited; herbs have been tucked under pillows at night in the hope that dawn will reveal

true love. And throughout the ages, in all religions and cultures, flowers are invari-ably present when two hearts are joined together by the nuptial vows.

Intertwined with the bride's tresses, clutched in her pale hands, draped as leis around her shoul-ders, pinned to her gown, or cradled as a sheath over her Bible, flowers are part of the special day. All flowers become rich in sym-bolism when held in the bride's hands. And yet, not content merely to trust vague interpretations, the romantic Victorians embellished the secrets that petals whisper. They fashioned a language of flowers used in a coy correspondence between lovers, which, when the flirtation was complete, crept softly into the bride's bouquet. Those blossoms intermingled in such incomparable poetry that even now brides borrow from the language of flowers. Scattered here and there, hidden in a bouquet or buttonhole, is perhaps a sprig of heliotrope for devotion, festoons of ivy for fidelity, the perfumed throats of tuberoses for mutual affection, airy sprays of handsome white heather for future fortune. All shades of sentiment can be fashioned in buds.

Acacia is the flower of friendship, ambrosia speaks of love returned, agrimony is the herb of gratitude, lily of the valley signifies happiness, and larkspur is the blossom of levity. But flowers are not the only eloquent element of a bouquet; fillers and foliage also hold meaning. Tendrils lightheartedly point to the person for whom the message is meant. Thorns hint at life's little snags while maidenhair speaks of the diplomacy and discretion so necessary in a relationship. Rosemary is the herb of remembrance, especially valued among friends; since biblical times myrtle is a token of love; and sweet laurel stands for constancy. Unforgettable, an herb's message also floats on the heady aroma that wafts from every leaf, exhaling the perfume of dreams. Petals speak the language of love often more eloquently than do our lips.

$\mathcal{T}$HE BRIDAL PARTY

Maid or matron of honor, bridesmaids, junior bridesmaids, flower girls, ring bearers, and train carriers ~ a wonderful world of options exists for you as you choose the members of your wedding party.

A natural starting point is the selection of the maid of honor or matron of honor. Her very pleasant responsibilities may include supervising the floral arrangements, making sure every rose, every lily is at its freshest. You may want to rely on her to shepherd

young flower girls and ring bearers. And at formal weddings, the maid of honor might wish to be in charge of arranging the bride's train in delicate folds. As a reflection of her elevated status, her attire will have an extra element of elegance, such as more elaborate flowers, headdress, or jewels than the bride's other attendants.

The role of the bridesmaid has its roots almost as deep in time as the marriage rite itself. In ancient civilizations, members of the bride's and groom's families would help prepare the bridal costume and accompany the bride to the ceremony. But it was during the socially conscious Victorian era, when manners and etiquette seemed to be elevated to an art form, that the role of the bridal attendant became much more prominent. Dressed in gorgeous wedding finery, looking almost as beautiful as the bride herself, bridesmaids eagerly shared in their friend's happiness. The wedding had become a showcase for lovely, unmarried young women to display their special qualities before the eligible bachelor friends of the groom. Thus, being a bridesmaid became regarded both as an act of friendship and a sign of good luck.

In Victorian days, as now, the bride was free to select as many attendants as she wished. Her only limitation was the availability of male escorts in the wedding party. And while the traditional image of a bridal party is of a happy group of young people, it is charming to express friendship by involving all those who are special, young and old alike.

At the height of Victorian era, it was the custom to dress bridal attendants in identical outfits, often in a gown that was an exact replica of the bride's ~ even to the point of wearing a veil. In 1840, Queen Victoria's eleven young bridesmaids wore white satin gowns similar to hers, but with-

out her veil of English lace. In the late 1890s, bridesmaids' gowns became more and more modest. As a result, the bride's beauty and fashion occupied the spotlight, and she became the focal point of the wedding party, as most brides would agree she should be.

Today, while it is unusual to see a bride and her bridesmaids dressed in the same style gown, so lovely is the all-white wedding that it remains a classic choice, perfectly beautiful at a formal or informal gathering. But most brides draw from a wider palette in selecting colors for their bridesmaids, choosing tones from the same color family to harmonize with bouquets, hair coloring, and the bridal ensemble itself. Baby-soft pastels seem to be perennially popular as they work superbly with the subtleties of

The glow of pink as soft as an apple blossom illuminates two bridesmaids. Both exemplify the finesse that simple styling, fine tailoring, and one perfect bloom can produce.

◆

delicate jewelry and creamy flowers to create a soothing tableau for the occasion. But why stop there, when there are such wonderful shades from which to choose: washes of champagne, ecru, ivory; rich earthy tones for a fall wedding evocative of a golden harvest, greens mossy and fresh for spring, winter whites accented with bold colors that remind us of flowers in the snow. Strong, vivid tones provide an extra measure of glamour and make the bridal outfit even more striking. "The purest and most thoughtful minds are those which love color the most," declared John Ruskin in 1852. Since this is a day for high emotion, not restraint, show your true colors.

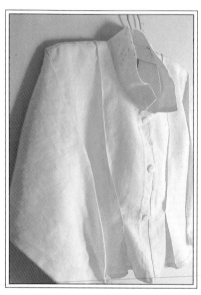

Untraditional choices for the bridesmaid include this beautifully tailored vintage blouse, above. Opposite, a toe-length skirt of silk is paired with a soft linen blouse in a peach tone.

Whatever their style, whatever their color, the most pleasing bridesmaids' dresses are those that echo the feeling of the wedding: Light summer days and evenings are made for a dreamy look; long filmy dresses of linen and lace evoke a turn-of-the-century mood and seem as fresh and sweet in the morning as they do later at the reception. Late afternoon calls for more adornment, so out come the laces, trims, ribbons, beads, and bows, paired with full-skirted dresses plumped up with petticoats and crinolines. Hand-crocheted gloves, small Victorian purses or fans, high-button shoes, rosebuds held in place with combs of silver, faux ivory, or tortoiseshell continue the playful look. More formal ceremonies, evening parties, and midnight suppers suggest bridesmaids in floor-length satins, taffetas, silks, and moirés, usually as an echo of the bride's style, yet less grand and elaborate. The perfect accompaniments are lush cascades of flowers, jewels and ribbons woven

through the hair, and high-heeled satin slippers for endless dancing.

❖

To dress up in fancy clothes, to carry beautiful flowers, to do an important job, and to have everyone notice how poised you are ~ to be a flower girl is every little girl's dream come true.

Children add a special charm to weddings ~ perhaps no more so than the flower girl. And if there is more than one candidate for this very special spot? A pair of flower girls, a trio, or a quartet will only increase the loveliness of the day. It is hard to imagine anything sweeter than a chorus of serious little girls dressed like the innocents of Kate Greenaway drawings in their perfect cotton frocks and long white pinafores.

In Victorian days brides were usually attended exclusively by a group of three

A flock of flower girls rushes down the church steps moments after the ceremony. The charming variety of dress styles is unified by color and accessories: lacy white gloves and stockings, halos of pink and white roses. Rustic baskets laced with vines are filled with petals to toss at the bride and groom.

◆

or four young girls who acted as brides-maids, a custom still followed in many European weddings today, certainly in British royal circles.

While flower girls in modern wed-dings play a different role, they always look heavenly, whether dressed simply, perhaps in cotton or linen, hair crowned with single wreaths of small precious flowers such as honeysuckle or rosebuds, or out-fitted more for-mally in floor-length dresses of silk or satin. A group of flower girls looks beauti-ful in contrasting colors, in soft pastels, and in shades of white and the freshest cream. They may be wearing straw hats rimmed with meadow flowers and streamers of satin ribbon. They may carry tiny bas-kets of pansies, nosegays of violets and lace, handfuls of perfect rosebuds, or a little fistful of Queen Anne's lace tied

Left, a perfectly composed little angel wears a peerless organdy gown as light and airy as delicate meringue. Above, tendrils of flowers gracefully weave their way through the well-behaved tresses of this sweet child.

with French ribbon. Some brides love a plain, rustic look and have flower girls carrying watering cans filled with just-picked garden flowers. Whatever they carry, it should be easy to hold and not too fussy. Even little cherubs are known to become distracted sometimes.

At ceremonies in ancient times, children would throw herbs in the path of the bride and groom as a symbol of good luck, pros-perity, and fertil-ity. This custom is still followed today as flower girls toss rose petals in the air following the ceremony. At Victorian wed-dings, young children would pass out tiny nosegays and boutonnieres of the bride's favorite flowers to guests. Besides giving the flower girl a very spe-cial job to do, this is one of the nicest ways of honoring each guest and making the experience more intimate.

Nattily attired for a summer wedding in seersucker knickers and knee socks, with suspenders just like his father's, or wearing a suit and tie for the very first time, the ring bearer looks so winsome dressed like a little boy rather than like a miniature adult. Unfussy clothes are best this day, and they hold their appearance throughout the ceremony and reception. Woolen trousers or shorts in navy, charcoal gray, or black are wonderful with cotton shirts and bow ties. This attire can strike just the right note at both formal and informal weddings.

While it is traditional for the ring bearer to carry the ring on a pillow, for very young boys carrying anything extraordinarily frilly could encourage mishap or insurrection. Instead, a small velvet heart, with the ring or rings firmly attached, or an easy-to-carry basket with rings safely tucked inside, might be more prudent. Success will be enhanced if the young ring bearer is quietly shown what is expected of him and not asked to do anything that makes him uncomfortable.

The informality of stripes and seersucker is often the best choice for little ring bearers, opposite. The flower girl above, is poised in a formal organdy dress.

◆

In many weddings, two little boys are chosen to be train bearers. It certainly is a tender sight as the bride seems to float down the aisle with the help of these handsome young fellows. In this scenario, dressing the train bearers in similar outfits makes a strong presentation. Dark colors are dramatic here, providing a striking contrast with the whiteness of the bridal gown.

After the serious emotions of the ceremony, young members of the bridal party should be permitted to relax. Letting their natural good spirits come to the surface will only heighten the sense of celebration.

Traditionally, the mother of the bride is the most important woman next to the bride. No longer exercising the iron grip that Victorian mothers had over their daughters' weddings, today's mother is more of a friend to her daughter as she shares in the excitement of the big day. Together, they pour over guest lists, draw up menus, discuss the merits of orchids over calla lilies, and wonder where the family's silver coffee urn might be.

For her wedding-day outfit, silks, satins, laces, and cashmeres will bring out her delicacy, and well-chosen accessories will provide the perfect touch of color and polish. A pearl choker is just right with her high-necked dress, along with kid gloves for the church and a good supply of lace handkerchiefs inside an antique embroidered bag. A classic hairstyle ~ upswept, French-braided, or knotted ~ and sophisticated perfume and makeup are all a part of the mother of the bride's artistry. She might choose her outfit in a soft color ~ dove gray, mauve, or off-white ~ or toast the new couple wearing bold copper, russet, or gold. While shorter skirts are fine all day, long skirts look wonderful from noon on.

A classically pleated *white charmeuse gown, banded in rhinestones at the waist, makes an elegant choice for the mother of the bride.*

◆

Weddings can be occasions to honor all the women in the family. What could be lovelier than small bouquets of flowers waiting at the table for the mothers in both your families. Your new husband's mother, soon to be a big part of your life, will be touched by the thoughtfulness of

an extra-special floral tribute that lets her know how dear she is to you.

$\mathscr{A}$ FINE TROUSSEAU

A traditional bridal trousseau extends far beyond beautiful lingerie and delicate under-garments. It includes all the personal items ~ toiletries, dresses, coats, jewelry, and footwear ~ the bride would need for herself, as well as a massive supply of linens for her new household. Long a major pre-occupation of mothers in the eighteenth and nineteenth centuries, the task of

$\mathcal{V}$ictorian ladies wore special "combing" gowns when they dressed their hair. This bride's antique cotton gown is made of intricate crocheted panelwork. Her upswept hair, fastened with antique hairpins, looks lovely with drop earrings of luminous pearls.

◆

assembling a trousseau would begin soon after the birth of the child. Because of the precious, time-consuming quality of hand-made finery, collecting a substantial trousseau could easily be a lifetime's work. And as the tablecloths, sheets, and linens

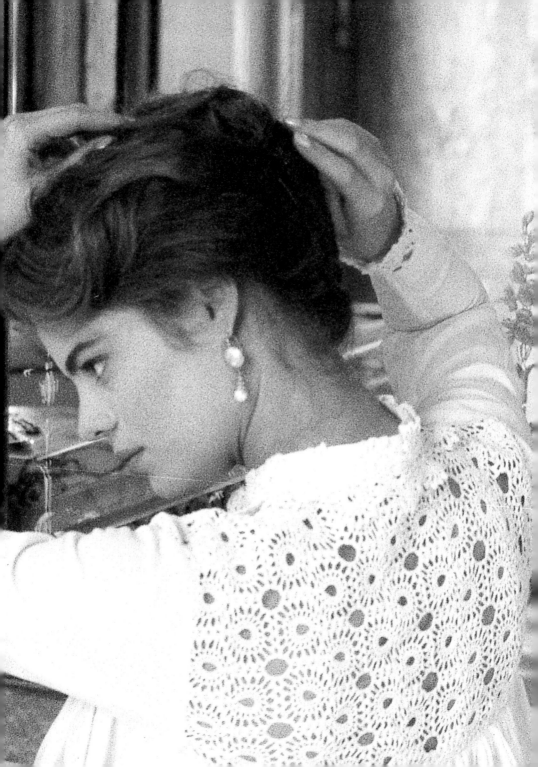

mounted up, a place would be needed to store the trousseau ~ thus giving birth to the hope chest, a well-named piece of furniture wherein the future bride's household needs and hopes would reside until her wedding day. Up until the end of the nineteenth century a trousseau (from the French word *trousse*, meaning "little bundle of sticks") for a proper Victorian miss would consist of "twelve of everything": nightdresses, knickers, chemises, stockings, gloves, hankies. In addition she would depart for her new home and her new married life with enough breakfast gowns, tea gowns, day outfits, evening attire, and outerwear to see her through many years.

No longer the sole domain of the bride's mother ~ and the expense of the bride's father ~ today's trousseaus are often assembled from shower and engagement gifts. Frequently, the smallest items become the most treasured: a lace handkerchief embroidered with the couple's initials, gloves of silk, brocade dance slippers.

Starting the wedding day at a dressing table laden with fine toilette accessories will heighten the bride's excitement ~ cut-crystal jars with engraved silver lids holding face powder; an ornate silver brush and comb set, perhaps a gift from the groom's godparents. Strands of creamy pearls spill provocatively from their ancient velvet case. A cotton camisole freshly laundered and perfectly pressed sits primly inside a linen lingerie case. Lalique atomizers of favorite perfumes mingle with jolly fat powder puffs. A glorious day is about to begin.

A delicate lace dressing gown, above, awaits the bride. Left, a last-minute check in the mirror reveals all is perfect ~ dress, hair, jewelry, and flowers.

Chapter 3

WITH THIS RING

nce you start to sketch out your wedding plans, you will start thinking like a twosome, peeling away layers of politeness and others' expectations to discover what you both want, from the solemn wording of your vows to a myriad of more earthbound considerations, such as guest lists and seating arrangements.

Creating a memorable wedding requires a deft hand and diplomacy. The first important decision to be made is setting the date ~ will it be heavenly day in summer? Or is yours a romantic soul that always envisioned a wedding at Christmastime? You might love the promise of spring and can imagine pots and pots of hyacinths, crocuses, tulips, and narcissus, their heady scents guiding you down the aisle. There may be practical considerations to honor ~ family schedules and work commitments ~ or you may want to wait until all the maple trees outside the chapel in your hometown turn a blazing yellow.

After the date has been set, your thoughts turn to finding just the right place to suit your mood. Possibilities can range from lifelong dreams to spur-of-the-moment whims ~ a tiny stone chapel framed in honeysuckle, a glorious cathedral where hundreds can witness your vows, a mountaintop where earth meets sky, or the library of your alma mater, rich with oriental carpets and presided over by leather-bound volumes you have always loved. The colonial herb garden at a local historical estate may be your notion of love in bloom, where you plight your troth under a trellis arch covered by clematis, or a spare elegant loft where the notes of a string quartet soar as high as your heart. Perhaps you want to be married at your family's home and fancy the idea of vases of rhododendron, amid platters of Virginia ham and biscuits, waffles and red-eye gravy at noon.

The spirit of each season becomes a glorious background for a wedding canvas. Opposite, the freshness of spring, with its whispers of blossoms and leaves, lends a special grace, while summer's sublime garden bounty, above left, is a quiet joy in sunlight or cool shade, At the heart of autumn, below left, are colors blazing with a jewellike intensity.

❖

woman, the past with the present, individual souls with the greater cosmos. Many couples embrace this notion as a way of deepening their experience.

Each season of the year brings with it a special quality that becomes a part of the wedding. The gift of spring is renewal in its giddy show of tulips, daffodils, dogwood, and lilac, in its warming days and longer nights. The couple that marries in the spring has a new beginning every bit as promising as this flowering season. Summer with its offhand elegance provides a magical back-

But beside its sentimental appeal, the wedding site has a spiritual dimension that can often be overlooked in the busy activity of wedding preparations. Various cultures consider it to be a sacred place, where man is united with drop from sunrise to moonrise. Meadows of wildflowers sway in warm breezes, waiting to be made into daisy chains by young guests; afternoon light turns to a benign glow as crickets usher in early evening. Even cities are imbued with this sensation of time standing still. A ceremony in summer can be filled with glorious contrasts: the seriousness of the vows, the gaiety of the event, the heat of the sun, the cool interior of the church; the bride in formal wedding dress, flower girls running barefoot across lush green lawns.

Autumn, on the other hand, is like a brisk tonic, awakening summer-lulled senses to change: Green leaves turn to gold and red, mellow breezes become crisp, gardens are ready for harvest. The Thanksgiving season offers a bounty of mums, kale, ivy, pumpkins, Indian corn. A wedding at this time of year acknowledges the gifts given to us all.

The Christmas wedding has a powerful hold on our imagination. What a wonderful confluence of events! The celebration of the holiday, with all its attendant joys and gift-giving, is a time of extravagance and a time for love. The whole community may join in rejoicing at this happy event. Churches are dazzling with the season's bounty: boxwood, myrtle, ivy, vines of all sorts entwining altars banked with pots of precious ruby-red flowers to signify birth: deep red amaryllis, cyclamen, red roses, poinsettias. Purity is symbolized by a softly hued palette of whites: lilies, orchids, chrysanthemums, freesias, French lilacs, and paperwhite narcissus. Hundreds of votive candles reflect the brightness of both the season and the wedding celebration. Wreaths and garlands hang from every doorway. For the ceremony, perhaps topiaries of rosemary will stand at attention at the end of each pew, in terra-cotta pots dressed with huge red velvet bows.

Snow blankets the ground in purifying beauty, preparing it for the Christmas bride. Opposite, on a church in New England, a pair of simple evergreen wreaths on holly-red doors announces the joy of this double celebration.

◆

Children are always a major part of Christmas, and they can be a delight at a Christmas wedding as well. You can play Santa to as many little ones as you like by including them in your party ~ flower girls and ring bearers, adorably dressed in wedding-best laces and woolens. They fuss at the doorway, like colts straining to bolt from the box. The flower girls' excited little hands hold baskets of red rose petals ~ they can't wait to fling them at the newly-weds after the ceremony. Guest after guest files into the church and fills up the pews, one side for the bride, one for the groom.

Nothing brings so much satisfaction as knowing how much you have done to make this setting beautiful. Everyone's spirits are heartier, everyone's emotions are more openly expressed at this joyous "double" celebration.

WEDDING MUSIC

Wedding programs are opened and eyes closed as the haunting melody of Ralph Vaughn Williams's "O How Amiable" floods over the church, splendid in its wedding raiment. A mood of high romance is set as the maid of honor gracefully arranges the bride's veil and train in the vestibule before she makes her entrance to the Processional in G Major by Handel. Strictly traditional? By all means, but this may be a perfect reflection of the musical taste of the bride and groom, just as another couple might choose to start their ceremony with "Annie's Song" by John Denver.

Selecting your wedding music should be, above all, fun. Throw away those notions that it has to be predictable or stuffy and let your taste and imagination soar like the high notes of Placido

Domingo. One way to organize your thoughts might be to attend concert at a local music conservatory and have tea afterward with its director. Describe your service, its philosophy and tone, and before you can say "All You Need Is Love" you will probably see your wedding music taking shape. A research trip to the library could yield a wealth of cassettes. Take them along with you when you preview the wedding site to see if Johann Pachelbel's Canon in D Major works in a garden, or if Aaron Copeland's "It's A Gift To Be Simple" played on a flute fills the church.

A gentle feeling fills the air as well-loved hymns and songs are played on fine antique musical instruments. Their dignified beauty adds elegance to any ceremony.

◆

immediacy of the experience is as important as the expertise of the performer; your eleven-year-old niece playing Bach's "Jesu, Joy Of Man's Desire" on the church organ would be a memory you would always cherish. But should the place where you are marrying possess a quality sound system, your options can be greatly expanded to include the finest musicians, singers, and orchestras in the world ~ on tape: Imagine soprano Kiri Te Kanawa thrilling your guests with "Let The Bright Seraphim And Their Celestial Voices All Unite," just as she did for a royal wedding more than a decade ago. If you or your groom are a musician or vocalist, you might like to express a tribute to your beloved on a fine instrument or voice your sentiments in song.

When thinking through the ceremony, ask yourself if you would prefer live music or a recording of a major artist. Usually the strains of a violin or piano are far more moving played in person. The

$\mathcal{V}$OWS FROM THE HEART

You have picked a beautiful setting for your ceremony, have charming ideas about how to decorate it, and have planned every detail down to the last candied violet. During all the decision-making, you and your fiancé have been trying to imagine yourselves actually taking your wedding vows. Perhaps you have been quoting bits of well-loved poetry, thinking you could find a place for some of it in the ceremony. Maybe you have been hurrying home from libraries and bookstores, your arms loaded with volumes of Shakespeare's sonnets and other great love poems.

You might look for ideas and inspiration in other weddings you have attended. Visit a favorite old bookstore to discover the language in which your favorite poets and writers commemorated their marriage.

Early one morning, open the family Bible to see if a particular reading from the Scriptures gives voice to your feelings.

If you plan to marry in a religious setting, you are probably leaning toward a traditional ceremony. Most couples are more at ease with an established service, leaving little to chance. Still, even with in that framework, a wide range of options can be incorporated to make religious vows even richer with meaning, such as blending them with selected hymns, prayers, poetry, and literary passages that hold great significance for the two of you.

If yours are two poetic hearts that seek the satisfaction of creating a wedding tapestry all your own, why not present each other with small journals and promise to write down any thoughts or passages you have read that you might

Favorite biblical passages come from The Book of Ruth and Letter to the Corinthians. Literary passages, both poetry and prose, provide other sources of inspiration.

◆

later sculpt into your own completely unique and personal vows.

$\mathcal{S}$CENES FOR A MARRIAGE

$\mathcal{S}$pires soaring to the heavens, old slate walkways worn with smooth with the footsteps of parishioners, wide front doors welcoming all ~ for most couples the most popular choice of a place to be married is still a house of worship. From whitewashed clapboard churches in the country to towering cathedrals and historic synagogues, all are sanctuaries. Within their religions, all are considered to be sacred spaces in which the marriage union may be blessed. But the couple who wishes to have a religious wedding need not feel bound solely to a such a setting. While some religions do not consider sacraments portable and limit ceremonies to a house of worship, today more and more clergy are delighted to perform wedding ceremonies in a variety of settings that are in harmony with the spirit of the day. What about the place where you fell in love? How lovely it would be to marry there, or in the conservatory of a botanical garden, or in a sun-filled ballet studio, the beauty of the day reflected over and over in walls and walls of mirrors.

For many couples the perfect choice is City Hall or a justice of the peace, sometimes for expediency, sometimes because they are too private to share such an intimate occasion in a public way. Others find the quiet and grace of a simple ceremony in a judge's chambers to be to the ideal frame for their wedding portrait.

Whatever the choice, there are infinite ways to enrich and personalize the marriage ceremony, from the vows you choose to speak and the music you select to play to the readings you share and the flowers and other grace notes with which you invest the room.

You and your fiancé may arrive at the ceremony in your prized vintage Ford, or you and your flower girl may step out of a pony cart. Jubilant chords of Mendelssohn's "Wedding March" may announce the wedding processional, or a soul-stirring tune by George Gershwin may set a highly personal and contemporary mood. The ceremony may be intensely solemn, with poems by Elizabeth Barrett Browning, John Keats, Emily Dickinson ~ or lighthearted, with musings from Mark Twain. As a gesture of goodwill and affection, parents, sisters, brothers, and other family members may wish to be included in the ceremony, either by speaking words from their hearts, or sharing the wisdom of a favorite reading, hymn, or poem.

The traditional presentation of the bride is one element that you might like to expand upon. Besides walking down the aisle with your father or a father figure, you can link arms with both your parents,

The unbearable beauty of light is filtered through stained glass and pours through the windows of an elegantly simple church in a small Connecticut town.

or you can make your way to the altar together, hand in hand. You might even create an honor guard composed of members of both families.

The exchange of wedding rings is another part of the service that invites creativity, perhaps a moving poem accompanying the traditional "I dos." As the ceremony concludes, a special prayer of thanksgiving might be invoked. In addition to expressing gratitude for their own good fortune, a gracious bride and groom can acknowledge the contributions of family and friends and request that they share in the blessing that the happy couple has received this day.

It was a lovely custom in the nineteenth century to give guests beautiful wedding programs detailing every aspect of the ceremony that was about to take place. You can perpetuate this tradition by creating one for your own ceremony, engraved or handwritten on paper that matches your wedding invitations. It should outline the service from the processional to the recessional along with the date, time, place, and participants. To make the program even more of a keepsake, you can embellish it with fine calligraphy, line art, or poetry. Add a fresh rose or a wash of watercolor for another charming personal touch. Arrange the programs in baskets by the church door, or ask your flower girls to distribute them to your guests as they arrive.

Before wedding preparations and anticipation snowball into one fabulous blur, arrange a quiet time for you and your fiancé to share your private thoughts on how to make even the most traditional of ceremonies a reflection of your personal selves.

Opposite, sunlight breaks over a bouquet of vibrant spring flowers positioned atop a pew. Above, lap robes bear an inconsiderate bride's signature.

◆

If you have planned a church wedding, thoughtful and imaginative decorations can underscore the beauty and feeling you bring to the service: The aisles blossom with seasonal flowers; bouquets tied with white satin ribbons cascade from the backs of the pews, while at the foot of each, tiny gardens of potted flowers and herbs announce that something wonderful is happening. At the altar, nothing could be lovelier than the floral bower that frames you in the gifts of the season ~ massive elegant branches from spring flowering trees such as quince and apple, fiery oaks and maples in autumn, scented pine and fir in winter. In summer you might cloak the altar in a christening of snowy white delphiniums, hollyhocks, and hydrangea. Your family Bible, placed on the altar and covered with the same beautiful blossoms, becomes a lovely personal note in the experience about to unfold.

The chuppah is one of the most visually compelling elements of a traditional Jewish ceremony. This protective canopy, held above the bride and groom, has been imbued with many symbolic meanings. Some believe it signifies a house in which the new couple will reside, or the entire world in which the they become "royalty" on their wedding day. Many believe it represents the sky of paradise. One poet has described it as "a table upon which we set our love as a feast, like a tent under which we work." It can be fashioned from anything from plain cloth to delicate lace. Often it is a light and airy trellis covered with flowering vines or lush flowers, or an enveloping forest of palms, ficus, or fir. In the high beauty of summer, a chuppah in a garden becomes a cool and

shady sanctuary that sheds its benevolence and beauty over the newlyweds.

$\mathcal{U}$NBOUND BY TRADITION

A religious wedding may be the stuff of many couples' dreams, but for those who prefer a less traditional setting, the choices are quite wonderful and varied. With no less joy and anticipation than the bride who plans an elaborate and traditional wedding, you may rush off to a justice of the peace in the countryside, or secretly decide on a lunchtime ceremony at City Hall. There, with nothing to distract you except the essence of the ceremony, you take your vows.

A wedding in a judge's chambers has an unmistakable aura of dignity. Perhaps the judge is a friend of the family, or an old school classmate. Surrounded by

$\mathcal{H}$istory and symbolism imbue the chuppah with exceptional beauty. This traditional wedding canopy is covered with ornamented silk; it is supported by four firm poles, each of which is surrounded by arrangements of fresh flowers.

◆

A Most
Romantic Setting

An invitation to a wedding at Seventy Hillside in Waterbury, Connecticut, is an invitation to romance. This elegant and stately Victorian mansion, originally built as a private home in 1901, is now a flourishing country inn with a new specialty ~ hosting ultra-charming weddings.

Whether a sweet springtime service in the hushed and fragrant rose garden or a winter celebration in the great old-fashioned parlor crackling with good cheer, this graceful home was born for romance. Its history of love started at the turn of the century, when the house was built as a wedding present to a young couple, John and Ella Shepardsom Goss, from both their fathers. The mansion itself was a gift from the bride's father, and the beautiful hillside site was provided by the groom's.

With a love as solid as the house's neoclassic architecture, the young couple

lived there throughout their married lives, raising their children in the grandeur of the house, complete with a music room, library, six bedrooms, playrooms, smokers, and more.

So beloved was Seventy Hillside that today the couple's grandson and his family live on the premises. They have even found a way to immortalize the very special qualities of this remarkable place by making it available to the pub-lic for wedding ceremonies and receptions. On the weekends, instead of teenagers' tennis rackets in the great hall, there are rose petals and rice. Where family pets once ran across the broad lawns, now barefoot flower girls and ring bearers play on the garden grounds. In the ornate dining room crystal goblets are filled for happy toasts. And once again this amazing home fulfills its enduring legacy of love.

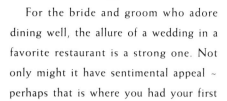

books in a wood-paneled room and clutching a lovely bouquet, you speak vows every bit as passionate as those uttered in a cathedral. And after the ceremony, you toast the day with vintage champagne served in crystal flutes you brought along. In these settings, there are many ways to heighten the intimacy that is the heart of the service. You can select and read a psalm or a poem you wrote yourself for the occasion. You might bring along a cassette of music you recorded especially for this moment. If yours is a giddy, spur-of-the-moment wedding, with no time to prepare, you might stop on your way to purchase the biggest bouquet of freesia you can carry. Afterward the two of you may splurge on a romantic meal at a celebrated restaurant or simply dash off with your best friends to dine al fresco in the park. Or perhaps a long walk, just the two of you, is all the celebration you need.

A long whisper of an organdy dress, opposite, seems made for a private ceremony. Above, a nosegay of pastel flowers and satin streamers is understated perfection.

◆

For the bride and groom who adore dining well, the allure of a wedding in a favorite restaurant is a strong one. Not only might it have sentimental appeal ~ perhaps that is where you had your first date, or where he proposed ~ but it offers an intimate setting and myriad luxuries.

Because every wedding combines serious moments with merry ones, a couple should look at restaurant space with an eye toward this dual purpose ~ for the ceremony, perhaps a nook created with lattice screens covered with flowers or old Victorian valentines, or a spot in front of a majestic floor-to-ceiling window under a bower created by tall vases of pussy willows or other seasonal blooms. There may be a beautiful fireplace where a hearty fire will wrap you in its glow as you say the words you have so carefully planned.

𝓜ARRYING AT HOME

Of all the places to be married, home has the greatest hold on our heart. Is there a bride who has not dreamed of drifting down garlanded stairs to meet her handsome groom? Lovely sentimental photographs ~ especially of their family weddings ~ are grouped in a galaxy of silver frames. Cherished childhood toys and talismans ~ baby cups, porringers, a beloved doll, a favorite teddy bear ~ are brought together from all over the house to witness the ceremony. Poignant notes from a piano or violin fill serene rooms clad in garden-fresh flowers. Best of all, the home wedding encourages everyone's participation, from older family members to the children, whose natural high spirits bubble over in familiar surroundings. At home, even your pets can join in the celebration!

𝒯here is truly no place like home for a setting rich in meaning and emotion. In this living room, the mantel glows in the nuptial finery of a swatch of antique lace and an artless arrangement of full-blown roses flanked by candlesticks that have graced this family through several generations.

◆

FROM THE BRIDE'S OWN GARDEN

If the kitchen is the heart of the home, the garden is surely its soul. You are truly fortunate if can have your wedding at home. Early on the morning of the ceremony, before the sun gets high, take secateurs in hand and harvest only the most perfect, dewy blooms. A purposeful ramble through the lilac garden yields masses of delicately shaded beauties that can be arranged in stately vases or float in silver saucers like potpourri. Bright black-eyed Susans, zinnias, and cosmos belong in bowls in shady corners to spread their color. Cheerful violets and pansies look sweetest in eye-level arrangements.

Garlands of ivy woven with dianthus, roses, stocks, and lamb's ears can be made in advance, kept in a cool, dark spot, then strung across doorways, arches, and

fireplace mantels a few hours before the wedding. Or flowers can be dried for an equally beautiful look.

Grace every room with the presence of flowers: On the powder room wall, pockets of aromatic honeysuckle draped around delicate hydrangea have an attention-getting quality. Living room, dining room, library, and study deserve special vines of autumn leaves, winter's pine, and boxwood. In the summer, tease guests with small nosegays of Queen Anne's lace and daisies lined up on a silver tray in the foyer as a welcoming gift. Loose stalks of meadowy canterbury bells look fetching in straw hats or baskets slung over the backs of chairs indoors and out. And what could be lovelier than baskets on kitchen counters overflowing with herbs, clematis, and dusty miller?

UNDER A SKY OF BLUE

The Victorians adored their botanical gardens, parks, and conservatories, and often planted gardens at home patterned after these glorious natural masterpieces. You may have always imagined yourself marrying in one of these beautiful settings, public or private ~ perhaps at cherry blossom time in the great allées of New York City's splendid Central Park, or in a graceful grove of birch trees at your godparents' country home. Or maybe you have always thought it would be great fun to wiggle your toes on the perfectly kept lawn of a great estate as you say "I do!" Wherever your heart pulls you, there are countless ways to make the occasion at once fresh, memorable, and very personal.

The lush all-white garden, opposite, was planted expressly for one bride's wedding. Above, a verdigris cupid provides a touch of romance in a public garden.

◆

Why not turn the event into a glorious picnic? Spread out blankets, plump up pillows newly covered in French country cottons, open wicker hampers, and dine on a wedding feast of baked salmon and crisp champagne. Carry a tussy-mussy of cabbage roses framed with a halo of heirloom lace and speak your vows " . . . under a sky/Of blue with a leaf-wove awning of green," as Thomas Hardy described it.

If you prefer a more formal mode, look for an estate that offers both exquisitely manicured grounds and a manor house in case festivities have to be moved indoors. Chairs and tables arranged in congenial groupings look welcoming on gravel paths, and serving tables dressed with plain white linens and simple flowers such as sweet peas are always elegant.

Chapter 4

DANCING
ON AIR

THEY DO NOT LOVE

WHO DO NOT SHOW

THEIR LOVE.

William Shakespeare

here is probably no more delightful a celebration
than a wedding reception. Whether as opulent as the wedding breakfast of Queen Victoria and Prince Albert in 1840, as dignified as an
afternoon tea held at a National Trust estate, or as poetic as a picnic
in a meadow of wildflowers, every wedding party stirs the senses,
excites the emotions, and touches the hearts of all assembled. Not
quite guests, not quite hosts, you and your groom are the centerpiece
of an ancient tradition born of hospitality and goodwill. With the
same thought and sensitivity that you brought to selecting your

wedding ensemble and flowers, you can create a celebration that will please and delight family and friends alike. Perhaps you have always dreamed of a highly romantic day, your silk gown rustling in the breeze on the verandah at a well-loved Victorian inn, heavy crystal glasses raised in a toast to you and your groom. If yours is a sophisticated spirit, seeking expression in a more formal mode, the regality of a sit-down dinner or elaborate buffet at a museum, estate, or gallery will sound just the right note. There are so many ways to make this day all your own, to make memories of dreams. Following a ceremony in judge's chambers, you can transform a private room in a restaurant into your own personal bower, or marry at home using fine family china, starched white tablecloths, and those funny silver dessert forks your mother loves so much. No matter what style you envision or and expense you feel comfortable with, the

reception is part of your first day as a wife. Now that is a day to treasure.

All senses come into play at a wedding reception. Guests may be greeted by the scent of fragrant garden flowers,

Tapers burn brightly as the on-coming evening cloaks the room in intimacy. Following a late-afternoon ceremony, guests are welcomed by the elegance of a champagne reception. Family silver and china frame a marzipan-topped wedding cake while crystal champagne flutes stand at attention, awaiting the bridal toast. Off in a quiet corner, gifts wait patiently to be opened.

◆

than at such an occasion, when all emotions are heightened. From soothing, soft background music to a recital that commands our full attention, from beloved songs that speak of our ethnic pride and heritage to foot-tapping dance tunes, the music you select for this day will become another mirror of your romantic values and ideals.

When planning your musical program, above all listen to your heart. Honor the musical passions that you and your husband share. Do you both love moving Irish ballads? You may wish to engage a harpist or young singer from a nearby music college. If dancing has made you closer, a four-piece group could keep you both in the clouds for hours. The only rule is to choose the music that resonates most with you as a couple. As Lord Byron observed, "All who joy would win

the lilting sounds of flutes, or the crystal-clear purity of chimes. But it is music, with its unparalleled ability to both express and inspire feeling, that can set the mood of your party. The effect that music has on us is at no time more potent

must share it/Happiness was born a twin."

Since music has such great power to create a mood, it often makes good sense to orchestrate the sequence of selections, bearing in mind the duration of the party, as well as its location, the time of day, the season of the year, perhaps even the preferences of your guests. A fanciful meadow wedding requires a great deal of preparation, but think of the joy generated by the sweet sounds of fiddles, flutes, and other instruments played heartily in the open air. What great fun it would be if you or your husband joined in by playing or singing yourself.

Spacious, light-filled rooms and lofts respond wonderfully to the ethereal elegance and serenity of a string quartet playing Vivaldi or the shimmering notes of a pianist playing Debussy. Late-day weddings, especially midnight suppers, always seem more sophisticated, so a more traditional group romancing the room with classic tunes from Cole Porter would fit in perfectly with the spirit of the celebration. A vocalist whose style and musical interpretation reflect your taste, from sophisticated cabaret songs to rousing ethnic tunes, could be a fine choice to fill the air at your reception.

You and your groom might enjoy researching other family weddings and drawing up a repertoire of music of these celebrations. These special selections from your family histories ~ including both your parents' favorites ~ could then be re-created at your own wedding. What a moving way to link past and present.

The imaginative bride can transform a pretty spot into a beautiful one with the stylish use of flowers. A visit to your recep-

140

tion site at the same time of day you plan to have your party will help you preview how it will look on that great day. Will it be bright in summer's light? That could illuminate the soft hues of flowers such as delicate old-fashioned roses gathered fresh from the garden. Will winter's pink sunset be turning to dusk, demanding additional lighting from soft clusters of candles placed to bring out the glow of fine silver nestled among calla lilies and phlox? Will it be a morning in early spring, when vases filled with forsythia and tulips look fresh placed all around the room? Will the floral choices look as charming in sun as they do in shade?

What is it about a winter wedding that seems so romantic? Is it the thought of a cozy indoors, candlelight and fires warming the soul? Long, elegant gowns of velvets and brocades, snowflakes of lace and bright satin sashes? Is it gentlemen in creamy white shirts and gold wedding rings, flowers on lapels, and Victorian things?

If you have an urge to marry in winter because you love the thought of romance, abundant offerings of this season await you. Look at the rich earthy hues winter provides ~ terra cotta, burnt sienna and umber, ruby reds, deepest evergreens, luscious ochers. Or cast an approving eye at the opposite end of the spectrum ~ opalescent white, creamy mother-of-pearl, blue whites of late snowy days. Golds seem so right now, too ~ pink gold, yellow gold, white gold, cloths shot through with gold, or whole wedding dresses of them, such as the one Harriet Vane wore to marry Lord Peter Whimsey in Dorothy Sayers's immortal love story "Busman's Honeymoon."

A young guest, above, provides an incomparable gift: a violin solo. Left, this beautiful sunlit reception room will soon be filled with the soothing sounds of a string quartet.

◆

From March to June, spring blooms slowly and offers the bride many seasonal delights. As each crocus and muscari push their way through the snow, daffodils blow in winds hot and cold, and clusters of violets are ready to fold into tussy-mussies. Bouquets from flowering trees look lovely on the wedding tables; long, full branches of dog-wood, quince, magnolia, witch hazel are all fine choices. Flowering fruit trees have their own special appeal, apples and pink cherries in particular. Old-fashioned garden standbys such as pussy willow, for-sythia, and rhodo-dendron become majestic in the hands of a creative bride. Lilacs, in lavender or French white, and even in the rarest yellow, all are incomparably beautiful and fragrant.

On the guests' tables, small pots of primroses, miniature narcissus, and

Every element of a wedding celebration deserves attention. Here, the bride's chair is dressed in a garland of fully open pink roses. Framed on an ivory underpinning, the garland is tied on to the back of the gilt chair with simple lace bows. Later it can be dried for a keepsake of the occasion.

hyacinths look fresh and hopeful. Azalea topiaries are elegant, as are flats of long-necked French tulips or frilly parrot tulips. Late spring and early summer offer dianthus, miniature carnations, and oriental poppies to wind into wreaths, weave around the stems of champagne bottles, or leave casually on tabletops.

Left, graceful branches from an early-flowering fruit tree demonstrate how beautiful just a single element can be. Above, an artfully complex arrangement looks as though it were just plucked from an English garden.

◆

For the bride who is limited more by constraints of time and budget than by imagination, one place to start is with dried flowers. The sky blue of bachelor buttons remains vivid; roses encompass a more vintage hue, their shapely figures staying intact. Baby's breath might even improve with age, as would clover and daisies. Violets in particular are a delightful surprise ~ when dried they are almost more endearing than fresh, papery and delicate but oh so winning. You can dry the flowers from your shower or family dinner, then make them into small arrangements. It is easy to imagine how much fun this project could become if you and your bridesmaids turned it into an afternoon tea party. It is always a good idea to make your centerpieces or ropes well beforehand to avoid any last-minute pressure.

A ROSE WEDDING

he bride who champions a single flower ~ the rose ~ as a symbol of love throughout her wedding day shows rare discernment. Magnificent enough to stand on its own, the rose has always evoked thoughts and images of heady romance and the deepest love.

The choice of roses is virtually unlimited during the four seasons: hybrid tea roses, old-fashioned garden flowers, the tiniest perfect rosebuds and miniatures, long-stemmed ladies, exquisite damasks, and antique moss roses, even vigorous climbers and ramblers. Highly scented or subtle, vividly colored or quietly elegant, tightly budded or full-blown, the rose offers a wealth of romantic possibilities. Fortunate indeed is the bride-to-be who can imagine wonderful ways to release this glamorous energy. Many begin their floral overture with their own bridal bouquets, striving for harmony and continuity with the style of the day. A clutch of creamy, mother-of-pearl—colored roses in full bloom will match the antique taffeta of a cherished family heirloom. A nostalgic

tussy-mussy of small pink rosebuds cosset-ted against old lace and tied with beautiful streamers is charming at a country wed-ding, as is an informal garden bouquet of sweet ramblers tied together with Queen Anne's lace. A glorious mass of pristine hybrids is in keeping with a more formal wedding. The bride might even play Cupid and perpetuate the love affair between roses and the ivy plant by mixing the two together in her bouquet and later rooting the ivy; planted among the roses in her garden, it becomes a living symbol of the growing love between husband and wife.

Flower girls and other young atten-dants fill small baskets with rose petals to toss at the bride and groom after the cere-mony. Baskets of roses hang from door-knobs to guide guests to the ceremony and reception, and mounds of champagne-colored roses cast their pearly sheen on sparkling crystal. At the cake table, the rose reaches its pinnacle as a halo of pastillage, or sugar paste, roses glows on the top layer of the cake. And for the groom's lapel, one perfect rose.

𝒯HE PERSONAL TOUCH

W ith an attention to detail, nothing has been left to chance this day ~ unless yours is that rare sensibility that loves a sweet disarray. Whether you plan to cut the wedding cake high atop a sky-scraper or at the foot of a brook, there is so much you can do to imbue the celebration with your own personality.

Because lighting plays such an important role in setting the tone and mood of any gathering, it should be one of your first consider-ations. Southern light can be beauti-ful filtered through a forest of palms in summer, potted firs in winter, or through clouds of netting. You can mute strong rays with inexpensive lace curtains that will create a fili-gree effect. A call goes out for can-delabra ~ so much softer than overhead lighting as day turns to early dusk. In summer, a late twilight envelops cele-brants in a highly romantic mood. Pools of votive candles would be exciting inside or on the stone balustrades of a verandah. Paper lanterns strung from trees always look so languorous blowing in gentle breezes.

Your next consideration should be how your guests will dine. Airy, ornate

𝒜bove, wrapped around a marble hearth, an exquisite cornerpiece of lilacs and roses is a tribute to the ingenuity of the winter bride.
Right, a silver candleholder alongside a bowl of lilies creates a charming tableau.

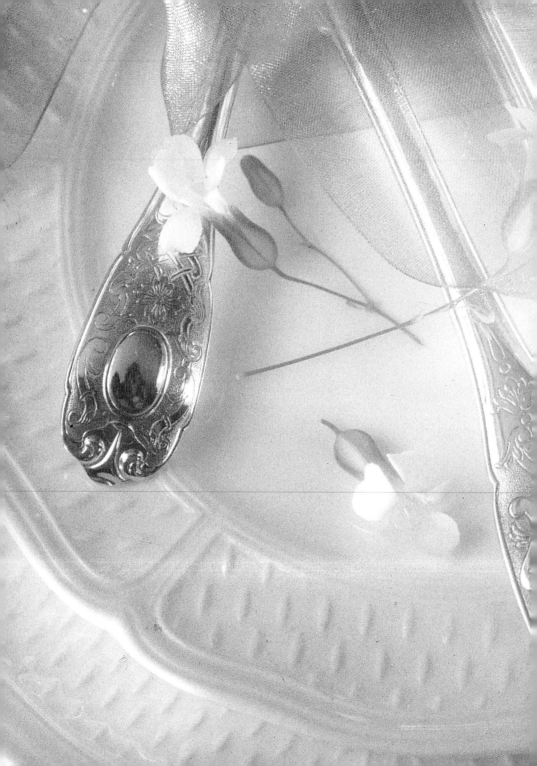

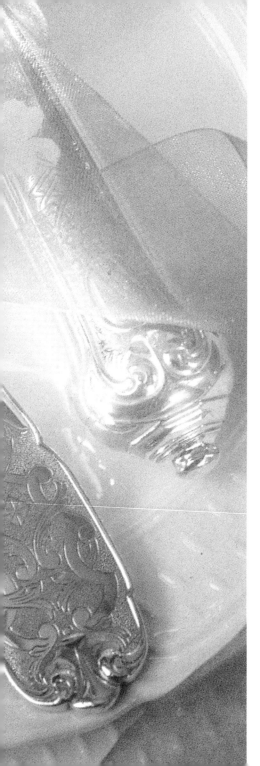

chairs and tables of ornamental iron add a Victorian flavor, indoors or out, and a love seat for the bride and groom is a charming alternative to traditional seating. Bamboo chairs, either gilded or in a faux finish, can look as right at breakfast as at midnight supper, and they can be moved around easily as guests regroup to visit with old friends. In high summer, rustic Adirondack chairs and wicker porch furniture are dapper arranged on a garden lawn.

A skillful hand blends old and new to bring out the best qualities of each: Antique silverware plays off delicate iron stoneware, the perfect backdrop for a dusting of French ribbon and pear blossoms. The bride even persuaded the sun to bathe the scene in a golden glow.

◆

Table settings are an opportunity for great artistry. If yours is a wedding that is strong in family tradition, you will want to incorporate as many heirlooms as possible. Out from family linen chests, china closets, and pantries come old friends: silver serving pieces, crystal silverware, and the linens you love so well. There is that perfect silver epergne ~ it will make an extraordinary centerpiece filled with cool green grapes, baby's breath, and kumquats. And the family punch bowl ~ it looked so big when you were a flower girl; wouldn't it be wonderful now wreathed in roses straight from the garden? And the silver dessert service ~ any ancestor would be proud to know it is being used to cut and serve the wedding cake at another family celebration.

Mentally scroll through the procession of dishes you would like to offer, matching serving pieces with food and mood: heavy silver for serious elegance,

Paired with heavy cut crystal, fine linens, and lace, these antique wire posy holders are a delightful surprise on two sumptuous wedding tables.

◆

pressed glass for delicacy, colorful painted stoneware for a bit of whimsy. A romantic theme says bring on all the precious and ornate silverware, dessert services, bud vases, and pitchers you can. They will look beautiful gleaming atop snowy white tablecloths. If you love a cozy Victorian feeling

but your guest list has grown beyond your china collection, consider using clear glass plates and blending in bits of Victoriana such as antique demitasse cups, so beguiling filled with nuts and chocolates. Footed candy dishes make strawberries look sensational, and anything at all in crystal looks old-fashioned, even those poor homely gherkins. At an outdoor wedding, baskets and wicker trays have great appeal. Fill some with rolled cloth napkins and enameled plates for a picnic spirit, others with fruit, cheeses, and tiny sandwiches. To evoke the feeling of four o'clock tea at an English estate like Brideshead, start with starched white linen, cucumber sandwiches, and tables set with Waterford crystal.

White linen has always been the traditional choice to dress party tables, perhaps because it makes everything look so crisp and fresh. But you are certainly not

limited ~ soft, muted pastels lend an Impressionist look when topped with masses of tulips, sunflowers, and rhododendrons. Linens can be anything from heirloom-quality laces to yards and yards of tulle you have just bought. Gathered in plump bustles, corners can be fastened with ribbons, bows, and streamers. Satin by the yard makes a shimmery glow for the late-night sophisticate. Put a crown of netting on top for a fairy-tale fantasy. Should you yearn for the spiffy look of a turn-of-the-century summer wedding, pastel-striped tablecloths add to the period. Fill tall galvanized florist's buckets with loads of flowers fresh from the garden and bank them everywhere for nonchalant elegance. Transform a private room in a restaurant into your own special place with starched white tablecloths and fine fami-

ly china. Sweet little bouquets of violets or nosegays of roses tucked into posy holders are endearing centerpieces.

There are so many ways to make the reception as personal as you wish, no matter what your style or budget. Place a gold-framed wedding certificate from an ancestor's wedding in an easel near the cake table. Or display the family Bible on top of a lectern for all to see. Drape your grandmother's shawl on a chair behind the cake, or hang a family quilt and surround it with tall branches of forsythia or dogwood. By winter's light, scores of tapers shed soft candlelight over the netting you have hung at the windows, arched over the doorway. Great ribboned baskets of homemade heart-shaped cookies wait on the lace-draped dessert table, daring anyone to resist them.

Antique napkin rings, opposite, and a precious silver dessert service with mother-of-pearl handles, above, demonstrate beautiful ways to incorporate family heirlooms in table settings.

SUMMER RECEPTION

"Summer afternoon, summer afternoon; to me these have always been the two most beautiful words in the English language," Henry James once said.

A bride's most beautiful two words may be "I do," but "summer afternoon" may not be far behind. The summer wedding reception is sheer heaven: Spirits seem free out of doors, flowers fresh, decorations light and airy. Every aspect takes on a buoyant feeling, as if by being in Nature's amphi-theater the seriousness of the day turns more lighthearted, though no less important.

In the bright warmth of a summer afternoon, you might want to plan for whimsy with an Alice-in-Wonderland look of delicate place settings, tea tables for small groups set under sheltering trees or beneath arbors of roses and honeysuckle. You can count on nostalgia with long trestle tables piled high with silver-footed dessert stands, lemonade in pressed-glass pitchers, long crocheted tablecloths bil-

lowing in the occasional breeze. Large oriental parasols can be opened to provide shade, or just for the fun of it.

On a summer afternoon, children will be gayer, their natural affinity with the outdoors making them unstoppable. Their antics and playfulness contribute greatly to the general merriment; their sweet wedding clothes make it all seem like a tableau from a Shakespearean romp. Nothing could be lovelier than the sight of little ones passing out blooms of hydrangea tied with satin ribbons or tiny nosegays of musk roses.

The summer reception invites Mother Nature as a guest, too, hopefully a well-behaved one. Keep refreshments cool and iced, whether in the shade or open air. To ensure a picture-perfect wedding cake, arrange it as if in a fernery, deep in shade, protected from light and heat.

As summer afternoon stretches on, the light remains. Daylight can last until ten o'clock at night, when, like weary children, it finally surrenders.

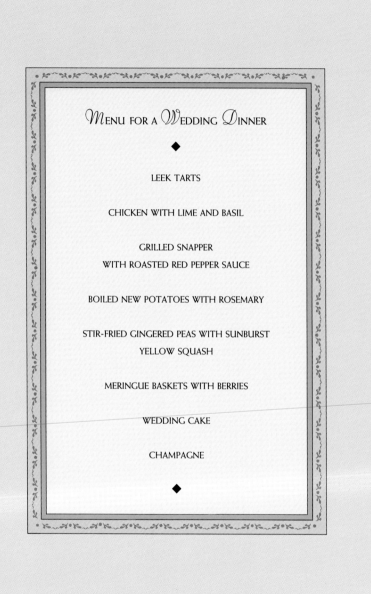

Menu for a Wedding Dinner

◆

LEEK TARTS

CHICKEN WITH LIME AND BASIL

GRILLED SNAPPER
WITH ROASTED RED PEPPER SAUCE

BOILED NEW POTATOES WITH ROSEMARY

STIR-FRIED GINGERED PEAS WITH SUNBURST
YELLOW SQUASH

MERINGUE BASKETS WITH BERRIES

WEDDING CAKE

CHAMPAGNE

◆

WEDDING CAKES

Vows have been made and rings exchanged. Now is the moment for one of the most beloved rituals of the wedding ~ the cake-cutting ceremony.

You and your groom have everyone's complete attention; whether the cake is rolled out on a cart to much fanfare or residing in a place of honor on its own flower-bedecked table, it is always the emotional centerpiece of any wedding celebration.

Fashions change and customs evolve, but the love affair with the wedding cake remains constant. As a symbol of sharing, it can be traced to ancient Greek ceremonies, when a cake of sesame seed meal sweetened with honey was offered as the final act of the wedding feast. Roman brides and grooms would first pay homage to their gods with cakes of wheat, then distribute this sweet to their guests. Centuries later, in Europe, the custom took the form of small, unleavened biscuits that were passed out to wedding guests. But it was not until the Middle Ages that these wedding "cakes" became one large cake ~ dark, heavy, and fruit-filled ~ of which all guests could partake. The eighteenth and nine-

If wedding cakes, like marriages, were made in heaven, they would certainly resemble this three-tiered beauty, festooned with swags and bows of rich buttercream frosting. Filigree scrollwork adds a baroque touch.

The rich cake on the left, with its rose tiara and filigree of piped buttercream frosting, seems straight out of a bygone era. On the right, delicate and whimsical petits fours with poured fondant icing resemble the small wedding cakes of old.

teenth centuries brought their own grandeur to the wedding cake, thanks to more sophisticated baking techniques and ingredients. The results are the elaborately frosted, multitiered cake creations we so love today. These became known as Bride's Cakes, and the traditional dark fruitcakes were called Groom's Cakes. To this day, when the bridal couple join hearts and hands to serve the wedding cake, they are reenacting a time-honored tradition rich with the hope of fruition, prosperity, and happiness.

When selecting your wedding cake, take inspiration from your fantasies; no longer are you custom-bound to serve a white layer cake with white frosting. Today's choices embrace a wide spectrum

$\mathcal{S}$weet raspberries and cream in a shell of airy meringue, left, make an excellent choice for a garden reception. The cake on the right, with its swirling swags and bows of Australian-method royal icing, just about waltzes off its silver platter.

of tempting confections ~ hazelnut, almond, apricot, orange, sour lemon, spice, Grand Marnier, mocha, burnt sugar, chocolate ~ even cheesecake, carrot cake, whipped cream cake, sponge cake, and pound cake. Do not hesitate to use strong flavors and fillings inside; they can provide a delicious counterpoint to the cake's sweetness.

With the tantalizing decision of the cake flavor behind you, the style and size of the cake are your next major decision. Will your cake be multitiered or a single layer; tall or wide; stately or humble; ornate or simple as a homemade strawberry shortcake at a farmhouse wedding? Draw inspiration from the theme of the day ~ a lovely, old-fashioned feeling would merit

THE MAGIC
OF CHRISTMAS

indows etched in lacy frost, tables covered with snowy tulle; the scents of pine, pomander, and rosemary: It is a Christmas wedding, the most festive, most exciting, most everything-you've-ever-dreamed-of time of the year. It is a little like marriage itself ~ two souls coming together to make one happy match.

This is the time for extravagance. Let every surface, every doorway echo your sense of festivity. Swags and garlands with seasonal boughs of Scotch pine and balsam let the spirit of Christmas intermingle with the joy of your wedding. As guests enter, they inhale the invigorating woody scent of winter. To heighten the romance, use the vivid colorings of the season's palette ~ deep red roses, anemones, amaryllis, cranberries paired against the greenery of holly, ivy, boxwood, and juniper. A dusting of sparkling gold makes antique ribbons, buttons, and bows. The pristine whiteness of vintage laces and veils looks lovely when combined with the whites of orchids, freesias, lilies, lilacs, and amaryllis.

Whatever time of day your reception is held ~ wedding breakfast, late-afternoon tea, midnight supper ~ it is sure to be imbued with the extra magic of the Christmas season.

a Victorian fantasy such as a rich genoise bedecked with cherubs, buttercream swags, flowers, ribbons, bows, and silver dragées. At a wedding such as this, the Groom's Cake can be the traditional dark fruitcake or his personal favorite, such as carrot cake. Perhaps you have always wished for a country wedding where simplicity is most companionable to your bridal finery and flowers. A high-sided cake with a smooth buttercream finish would be elegant crowned by baby's breath and tiny pink-tinged roses.

For a large at-home wedding, a towering, multilayered confection with ruffles, flourishes, and satin bows would be heavenly. A heart-shaped cake decorated with old-fashioned flowers straight from the garden would suit a more poetic mind. Certainly the simplest of home weddings would be beautifully complemented by a cake baked by the bride and friends from a treasured family recipe.

♂OASTS AND TOKENS

The centuries-old custom of toasting newlyweds with a flute of fine champagne has a double purpose ~ it confirms society's faith in the institution of marriage itself while it celebrates the passion the newlyweds hold for each other. We can thank the fun-loving French for this heady custom: At sixteenth-century wedding celebrations, a piece of toasted bread was placed on the bottom of a goblet. This special glass was then filled to the brim with wine and passed around among the ladies present. The lady who received the glass with the last quaff would also receive the morsel of toast ~ and the hope of good luck in finding her ideal mate.

No longer the sole domain of the best man, today's wedding toasts are made with equal elan by fathers, mothers, sisters, grandparents, and friends. It is especially thoughtful for a parent to dedicate a few words to his or her child on this day. A deeply moving description of a mother's hopes was written by Louisa May Alcott in *Little Women*. These words, penned over a century ago, are as beautiful today as they were then:

"I want my daughters to be beautiful, accomplished, and good; to be admired, loved, and respected; to have a happy youth, to be well as wisely married, and to lead useful, pleasant lives with as little care and sorrow as God sees fit to send. To be loved and chosen by a good man is the best and sweetest thing which can happen to a woman, and I sincerely hope my girls may know this experience."

Other traditions follow the toasts, including the tossing of the bridal bouquet or blue bridal garter, thought to bring good luck and a mate to the receiver. For the many brides wish to keep their bouquet, a "back-up" version becomes an appealing substitute, with no one the wiser.

A gracious, old-world custom still practiced by many new couples today is the passing out of bridal favors or keepsakes. Usually, bride and groom circulate together, distributing small gifts such as candies or flowers to each guest. This is still a charming practice, serving to bring the couple closer to each guest and allowing them an opportunity to give a small something back to everyone who has shared in their happiness. Nice ideas would be to fill a basket with small bunches of violets, or foil-covered candies wrapped in netting and tied with ribbon, tiny pots of shamrocks, packages of flower seeds, or pairs of creamy white candles tied together with laces of satin.

At an informal wedding, small terracotta saucers filled with a pincushion of rosebuds look lovely at each place setting; later, dried, they serve as a lasting memento of the day, as would a single rose attached to each guest's place card. Memories can also be sparked by tucking tiny cuttings of the nuptial nosegay at each place setting, or twining garlands of the bride's blossoms throughout the reception.

Borrowing one more custom from Victorian times, the bride may wish to give departing guests small boxes of Groom's Cake. Tied with white satin ribbons and heaped high on a table, this sweet memento can be given to guests as they leave the celebration.

Ready for the wedding toast: Delicate crystal stemware, filled with chilled champagne, is poised atop an antique silver tray.

◆

Chapter 5

$\mathcal{F}$ROM THIS
DAY FORWARD

Like exposed film in a camera waiting to be developed and looked at later, a wedding is an exuberant whirl of impressions and images. It seems as if only moments before you were folding the silks and satins of your trousseau, tucking pearls into the jewelry case your maid of honor sewed for you, making sure for the hundredth time that the secret gift you bought for your new husband is packed next to your perfume. Now you are shaking confetti out of your shoes and rose petals from your hair. And whether you are heading to your family's log cabin on the lake or to the railroad station for a journey across the continent, your destination is the same ~ a never-to-be-forgotten wedding trip.

Many people believe the word *honeymoon* derives from German folkways, an ancient custom of drinking a beverage made from honey for thirty days ~ one cycle of the moon ~ after the wedding. The Victorians called it the "bridal tour" and wrote at length about the proper trousseau and deportment for this harmonious occasion. At the turn of the twentieth century, *Harper's Bazaar* advised the bride to travel "in heliotrope cashmere, with bonnet to match." The young couple's departure was an emotional scene, for the bride was truly leaving in many ways ~ by marrying she was cutting her ties with home and was embarking on her own great adventure. As she was tucked into her carriage, the horses' heads decorated with wedding favors, a shower of old slippers would fly through the air to send the couple on their way. Today, of course, streamers are fashioned from shredded computer paper,

which our practical ancestors would have approved for its frugality while refusing comment on its provenance!

In Victorian and Edwardian days, it was not unusual for a couple to go off for two weeks, a month, or even more on a Grand

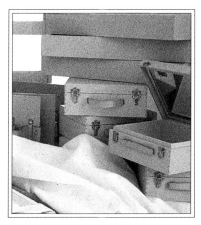

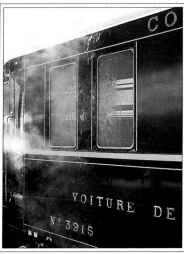

The journey is as important as the destination. Like the menu on the train, the "Do Not Disturb" sign, a watercolor of your new husband napping, memories are a part of the wedding trip you will always treasure. Pack plenty of pads for writing and sketching, a small camera, perhaps a journal to record these precious moments.

◆

the whack of croquet balls and the crash of ocean waves, these are places you might put high on your honeymoon discussion list.

For some, after the emotions of the wedding and reception, the best course of action is to avoid plunging directly into ambitious travel plans, at least for the first couple of days. Instead, head off to someplace quiet and recharge before your honeymoon trip. Pack your most comfortable sundress and walk along the beach, ride a carousel, nap in a hammock. You might even consider hiding out at home ~ just don't tell anyone! Stock the kitchen beforehand with plenty of champagne, caviar, and all your favorite takeout menus. As a special wedding gift for yourself, arrange for a cleaning service to come in while you are at the wedding so that when you clandestinely tiptoe

Tour of Europe or down to a seaside resort such as Cape May, New Jersey, or Newport, Rhode Island. These sun-filled resorts still retain their charming Victorian character. If your idea of heaven is lolling about in a rattan chaise longue listening to

home you will be greeted by a sight that makes absolutely no demands upon you.

SENTIMENTAL JOURNEY

Foremost in our imagination about great romantic getaways has to be a stay at a marvelous inn. Imagine elaborate, extravagant teas with strawberry jam spilling out of freshly made scones, savory sandwiches on homemade bread, ironstone teapots warm with bracing brew. The pleasure of this banquet, served on a sun-dappled terrace or an antique tole tray left outside your door, is heightened by the service, gracious and unobtrusive. You could not be more pampered.

What makes an inn great? Not simply its size; a small place with only two guest rooms on the banks of the Delaware River may be just as sophisticated and luxurious as a rambling shingled Victorian on the shores of Long Island's posh East Hampton. What makes an inn great is its sensibility, its dedication to hospitality, from fine linens and bedding to fireplaces lighted while you are out walking in the rain. It radiates tranquillity ~ no phones, no television, no faxes, probably not even a soda machine.

England, of course, is famous for its enchanting country inns, complete with

The stuff that dreams are made of: honeymoon sumptuousness in a regal, opulent setting. This utterly romantic room could be in New Orleans or on the Ile St. Louis, so elegant are its appointments.

◆

paths for long walks, high teas, sleepy villages with tiny cottages, peace saturating every idyllic hour. For the honeymooners, there are also visits to the inspiring homes of famous literary figures such as Jane Austen's cottage in Chawton, or sunny afternoons spent roaming through the great preserved country estates.

For visitors to France, few spots could be more romantic than Claude Monet's country estate, Giverny, with its breathtaking restored gardens, just a forty-minute train ride from Paris. Or go south on Le Train Grande Vitesse, which passes through Nîmes and Arles to the Côte d'Azur, each village more quaint and romantic than the next. Of course, Italy is a country that has always embraced lovers. What could be a more delightful honeymoon setting than the sun-drenched Mediterranean coast with its hundreds of hillside towns.

LIFE TOGETHER

A new husband and wife return from their wedding trip, and as they approach their home they see many different things. If they are tired from their journey, they see a haven promising comfort and rest. If they return refreshed, they see a happy place soon to be filled with laughter as they telephone their friends and family, renewing ties. Should they need nourishment, they see sustenance for the body and the soul. And as they cross over the threshold of their home, they see the beginning of another journey.

You may have had other homes, in other places, other lifetimes. You may have a larger world already in place ~ children from earlier marriages, family obligations. Yet your home feels different from the way it was before you married.

Every curtain you hang, every room you wallpaper, every painting you install is a delight. Small tasks become happy ones: arranging furniture, changing the linen closet. "What is more agreeable than one's home?" asked Cicero in 8 B.C.

One morning after your return, your writing box is brought down from its perch. Now a rush of affection speeds you along as you decide to take up your correspondence once again. Victorians loved the art of letter-writing, a passion that is especially understandable in this age of instant communication. Soon there is a stack of thank-you notes waiting for pretty postage stamps ~ notes to those who tailored your gown, arranged the church music, helped bake dozens of heart-shaped tarts. There are longer notes to aunts, uncles, parents, and friends who contributed so much to the success of your celebration. You may even want to tuck in a photograph of the two of you on your honeymoon trip.

*Signs of homeocoming:
A wicker suitcase waits to be unpacked after a honeymoon trip to a New England seaside resort, left. Above, lovely writing paper, perfect timing, and beautifully expressed sentiments lend charm to the bride's thank-you notes.*

◆

Now that the distractions of the wedding are past, this may be your first opportunity to unwrap and appreciate all your wedding presents. Fresh from their boxes come footed mirrors, crystal jars with sterling tops, enameled picture frames, needlepoint pillows, mother-of-pearl demitasse spoons. Reproductions of old family photographs in special frames, an antique bonbon scoop in swirling silver, a lace runner for the dessert table become part of your home. Before long, they have been transformed into beautiful tableaux above the mantel, on a bamboo side table, in the entry hall.

The togetherness of your new life is so surprising. The first major snowfall, and

off the two of you dash to make a snow-
man. Your husband surprises you with a
series of ballroom dancing lessons. You
take brisk walks at dusk, keep a cooking
journal of the new dishes you both love.
But the best part of the day is the
time you are
together at home
~ long lovely
hours spent read-
ing or at your
writing desk pour-
ing over herb
and flower cata-
logs, planning the
spring garden, or
sending catch-up
notes to friends.

*Weddings
are the best excuse for
dressing up your
home. Here fine flour-
ishes announce
a gracious sensibility
at work. With
all the panache of a
troubador's
bow, this luxurious
length of linen
is gathered up into
a glorious
sweep. Intricately
carved wooden
tie-backs hold the
summery fabric
in place.*

◆

Brides are
devoted to tend-
ing their homes.
With great heart
they arrange
crisp linens on
shelves, embell-
ish baths with fluffy towels and scented
soaps, hang lacy curtains at every window.
Certainly, couples do not always start out
with everything they need right at hand.
Some prefer to bring things in slowly,
choosing to live only with what has reso-

nance for them. Others would rather splurge on one great possession than have many small ones ~ an antique bamboo armoire with beveled mirror panels; a Chinese Art Deco rug; an ornate brass bed with the perfect patina of age; in the kitchen a Hoosier cabinet displaying Staffordshire or handmade pottery.

What you two start together now will have an importance that will grow in time, binding you closer. Begin a new collection, or add to an old one that you both prize. Enthusiasm of this type is contagious as you delight in surprising each other with great "finds" or in coming across the irresistible together. Learning as much as you can about your collection only makes the interest keener, the hunt more thrilling. Books and periodicals on the subject now crowd your bedside tables.

One-of-a-kind vintage bed linens give a home a personal touch. Crisp cool textures next to lacy filigree create a scene of tender serentiy. On the bedside table, a palette of white is surprised only by the buttery yellow center of the ranunculus.

♦

Your new togetherness may extend to adopting your first pet as well ~ goldfish in a delicate bowl, silver-throated finches whose warbling sounds provide a charming esprit, or something very emotional ~ the puppy you always wanted as a child or a kitten to purr you to sleep. Picking a name for your pet is part of the pleasure.

Magnificent or modest, any place where love is celebrated has a magnetic quality to it. Friends gather near and your social life takes on an added dimension. As you share friendships, your connection to each other is fuller, and stronger. Entertaining takes on a new cast as you eagerly put together the elements for your first dinner party ~ first, guest lists and menus; later, table settings and flowers. Little details can often be the most rewarding; you spend an afternoon designing the "perfect" invitations,

handwritten notes on heavy stock with frilly paper lace overlays.

When friends arrive, they are greeted by a new spirit in your home. You have brought out the poetry in everything ~ a welcoming wreath of lavender and bay leaves on the front door, the intimacy of a love seat next to the fire and a small tasseled ottoman at its foot. Even your party details have a festive dimension: You have set your table with the best and brightest of your china, silver, crystal goblets, and as a contrast to the heartiness of the wedding feast, you decide to serve lighter fare. One perfect menu might be herb cheeses, rustic bread, perhaps one great soup, and certainly chilled champagne in a silver bucket. The cheery warmth of candlelight illuminates your table, the strains of Vivaldi's *Four*

With the same hand as she would decorate her home, a new bride uses the spaces of a dollhouse-like curio cabinet, left, to express her personality. Above, a handful of roses in simple drinking glasses play off the heady blue hyacinths on the mantel.

◆

Seasons provide a soothing backdrop.

You find expression for your new, and renewed, sense of family by displaying the many photographs of your shower, rehearsal, funny moments with friends and family, your wedding and honeymoon. These can easily claim a photo wall or a shelf of their own, and always add interest and warmth to any room.

As a reminder of all the wondrous things you have done on your honeymoon, you assemble a collection of keepsakes. As the tissue paper flies through the air, you marvel at how perfect each treasure and trinket looks ~ seashells, the quilt you purchased on a whim, the miniature Lalique vase you found, just big enough for one perfect bud. To the observer, they may be no more than tokens. To you they are possesions valued beyond price.

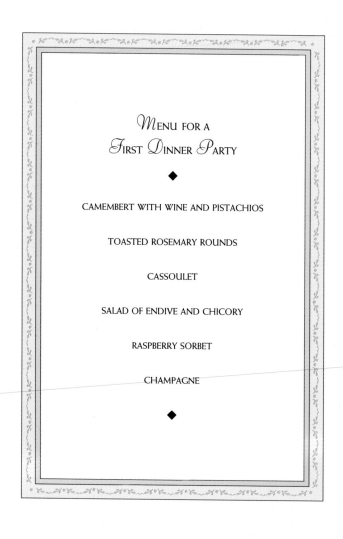

Menu for a
First Dinner Party

◆

CAMEMBERT WITH WINE AND PISTACHIOS

TOASTED ROSEMARY ROUNDS

CASSOULET

SALAD OF ENDIVE AND CHICORY

RASPBERRY SORBET

CHAMPAGNE

◆

ℰTERNAL KEEPSAKES

Afavorite gift for a newlywed couple in Queen Victoria's day was a specially designed wedding album. Leather-bound or covered in fabric, monogrammed with the bride and groom's initials or hand-embroidered with images of the flowers the bride carried, this album was treasured as the cornerstone of the new couple's wedding memorabilia. Inside its stiff board pages, was a wedding portrait ~ husband and wife, straight-backed and proud, looking directly into the future with determination. This was the official visual documentation of the occasion. If the couple was fortunate or well-to-do, additional photographs of the reception and family members might have been included. How intriguing to have a record of

Whether as sumptuous as this white moiré-covered beauty reminiscent of fancy Victorian candy boxes or as simple as a leather-bound family heirloom, the wedding album remains an eloquent and treasured reflection of the first days of a marriage.

◆

how your ancestors looked that day! What a connection you feel to them ~ your great-grandfather's strong features, your great-grandmother resplendent in the wedding dress she sewed herself, her cameo the same one you wore on your wedding day, her Bible the same one you held when you took your vows.

Rather than a prepackaged photography studio product with conventional poses, you may find it is much more satisfying to assemble your album from the photographs, verses, and drawings you have collected during this special time. Piece by piece, you create a visual history of the period between the day you decided to be married and your first day back from your honeymoon. Out of the wellspring of your creativity, you and your husband have a record that vividly illustrates your shared lives.

Another cherished bridal object many Victorian couples received was something that came from the marriage itself ~ their wedding certificate. Long before the advent of photocopying machines and computerized record keeping, these certificates were large, intricate, hand-colored works of art engraved with a host of cherubim, angels, flora and fauna. The vital statistics concerning the marriage were penned in with an elaborate, flowing Spencerian script, creating a document that became an instant heirloom.

One of the loveliest wedding presents that a bride can receive today is a hand-drawn replica of a Victorian wedding certificate, its information to be filled in afterward with calligraphy. An equally charming memento is a representation of the wedding vows illuminated on fine parchment. Colorful illustrations of the bridal flowers provide extra charm on this one-of-a-kind treasure.

If you are lucky enough to receive such a thoughtful gift, honor it with a hand-carved frame and a prominent spot in your new home. Every glance in its direction will bring back memories of your wedding day, an occasion so precious and special that Queen Victoria deemed it "the happiest day of my life."

The exuberance of the intricate Victorian wedding certificate was a celebration in itself. Since angels are timeless, this benevolent grouping could grace such a document today, becoming both a treasured wedding gift and future family heirloom.

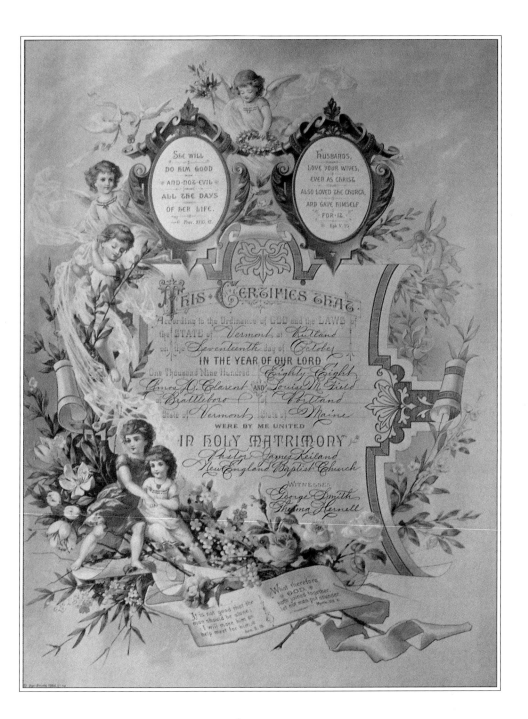

VICTORIA

$\mathcal{P}$HOTOGRAPHY CREDITS

Pages 90, 91 Photographs by Toshi Otsuki

Page 92 Photograph by William P. Steele

Page 93 Photograph by Toshi Otsuki

Page 94 Photograph by Elyse Lewin

Pages 96, 97 Photographs by Toshi Otsuki

Page 98 Photograph by Wendi Schneider

Page 99 Photograph by Tina Mucci

Pages 100, 101 Photographs by
Wendi Schneider

Page 103 Photograph by Wendi Schneider

Pages 104, 105 Photographs by
William P. Steele

Page 106 Photograph by Starr Ockenga

Page 108 Photograph by Elyse Lewin

Page 110 Photograph by John Kane

Page 111 Photographs by Toshi Otsuki

Page 112 Photograph by John Kane

Pages 113, 114 Photographs by Toshi Otsuki

Pages 115, 116-117 Photographs by
William P. Steele

Pages 118, 119 Photographs by John Kane

Page 120 Photograph by William P. Steele

Pages 121, 122-123 Photographs by
William Stites and Maria McBride Mellinger

Pages 124-125 Photographs by John Kane

Page 126 Photograph by Douglas Foulke

Page 127 Photograph by John Kane

Page 128 Photograph by Toshi Otsuki

Pages 130-131 Background photograph by
Jeff McNamara. Inset photographs, from
left, by Toshi Otsuki, Jeff McNamara, Jeff
McNamara, Joshua Greene

Pages 132, 133 Photographs by Toshi Otsuki

Page 134, 136, 138, 139 Photographs by
Wendi Schneider

Pages 140, 141 Photographs by Toshi Otsuki

Page 142 Photograph by Wendi Schneider

Page 144 Photograph by William P. Steele

Page 145 Photograph by Lilo Raymond

Pages 146-147 Background photograph by
Tina Mucci. Inset photographs, from left, by
Toshi Otsuki, Tom Hooper, Wendi
Schneider, Starr Ockenga

Page 148, 149 Photographs by
William P. Steele

Page 150 Photograph by Toshi Otsuki

Pages 152, 153 Photographs by
Hedrich Blessing

Page 154 Photograph by Luciana Pampalone

Page 155 Photograph by Tina Mucci

Page 156, 157 Photographs by Toshi Otsuki.

Page 159 Photograph by William Stites and
Maria McBride Mellinger

Page 160, 161 Photographs by
Hedrich Blessing

Page 162 Photographs, from left, by
Hedrich Blessing and William P. Steele

Page 163 Photographs, from left, by
Laurie Evans and Hedrich Blessing

Pages 164-165 Background photograph
by Wendi Schneider. Inset photographs,
from left, by William P. Steele and
Wendi Schneider

Page 167 Photographs by Wendi Schneider

Page 168 Photograph by Hedrich Blessing

Page 170 Photograph by Tom Hooper

Page 172 Photograph by Toshi Otsuki

Page 173 Photographs, from top, by Luciana
Pampalone and Nicolas Millet

Page 174 Photograph by William P. Steele

Pages 176-177, 178, 180-181 Photographs by
William P. Steele

Page 182 Photograph by Jeff McNamara

Page 183 Photograph by William P. Steele

Page 185 Photograph by Toshi Otsuki

Page 186 Photograph by Ralph Bogart

Page 189 Photograph by Hedrich Blessing

Page 192 Photograph by Toshi Otsuki